Keeping Strategy on Track

HBR Case Studies Series

Every day, managers face challenges that put them to the test. When it comes to the thorniest dilemmas, there's never just one right answer. Get the guidance you need from our new HBR Case Studies series. Straight from the pages of the *Harvard Business Review*, each book breaks down your most familiar—and formidable—business problems: you'll get six engaging scenarios, each with several detailed solutions by today's leading experts. Read the cases, gain more perspective, and hone your instincts—so you can finalize your plan and move forward successfully.

Other books in the series

Keeping Strategy

on Track

Harvard Business Press

Boston, Massachusetts

Copyright 2008 Harvard Business School Publishing Corporation
All rights reserved
Printed in the United States of America
12 11 10 09 08   5 4 3 2 1

No part of this publication may be reproduced, stored in or introduced
into a retrieval system, or transmitted, in any form, or by any means (electronic, mechanical, photocopying, recording, or otherwise), without the
prior
permission of the publisher. Requests for permission should be directed to
permissions@hbsp.harvard.edu, or mailed to Permissions, Harvard Business School Publishing, 60 Harvard Way, Boston, Massachusetts 02163.

ISBN: 978-1-4221-1469-8

Cataloging-in-Publication Data is available for this title.

The paper used in this publication meets the requirements of the American
National Standard for Permanence of Paper for Publications and Documents
in Libraries and Archives Z39.48-1992.

CONTENTS

Keeping Strategy on Track

Introduction

In *Alice in Wonderland*, Lewis Carroll provides no end of wisdom to business leaders. Consider the famous words of the Red Queen: "Here, you see, it takes all the running you can do, to keep in the same place. If you want to get somewhere else, you must run at least twice as fast as that!" (That sad fact of competition was the basis of a *Harvard Business Review* article called "The Red Queen Effect," by Stuart Kauffman.) Carroll's Duchess seems to have something of the executive coach in her—or at least the organizational psychologist's penchant for making the commonplace abstruse: "Be what you would seem to be," she states as her moral. "Or if you'd like it put more simply— 'Never imagine yourself not to be otherwise than what it might appear to others that what you were or might have been was not otherwise than what you had been would have appeared to them to be otherwise.' "

But perhaps Carroll's greatest business insight comes in the form of an exchange between Alice and the Cheshire Cat.

"Would you tell me, please, which way I ought to go from here?"

"That depends a good deal on where you want to get to," said the Cat.

"I don't much care where—" said Alice.

"Then it doesn't matter which way you go," said the Cat.

For businesspeople, the analogy is obvious, and so is the question it raises. What good is flawless execution, if it's only taking you more rapidly down the wrong strategic path? Deciding on the best way forward to serve the mission and profit goals of the company is the essence of strategy, and it's the problem facing every character in this collection of *Harvard Business Review* case studies.

Strategy as Story

Each month, the case study department of *Harvard Business Review* offers a short work of fiction centering on a business dilemma. Four experts in fields related to the issue at hand are then invited to provide their insight and advice.

In general, the format lends itself most frequently to "people problems"—the psychological knottiness of which can be better explored in a fictional example than in frameworks. Over several years of managing the case study department, however, I personally have become convinced that the format is just as valuable for exploring strategic issues. This is, in part, because it takes the aspects of management science that are in some ways most intellectually challenging, and makes them engaging. In a review of a "business novel"—*The Cure*, by Dan Paul (a former strategic planner for CEO Jack Welch at General Electric) and business writer Jeff Cox—*Publisher's Weekly* found the same kind of value. The book, it said, offered "a pleasant spoonful of literary sugar for business types who want to absorb the latest management trends." But beyond the sugar coating, the case's fictional format has a lesson to teach: that no part of business is free of people—and because strategy is left to the most powerful individuals in an organization, the drama surrounding it is all the greater. Strategic decision making, so often treated in the abstract and even numerically (think Porter's five forces, McKinsey's seven S's), is driven just as much by passions, biases, and all the dynamics that can develop between driven executives.

Chances are, your own organization is facing some of the same strategic issues as the companies depicted in these six cases, and the advice provided by the commentaries will be immediately useful. More long range, it's likely that in the course of a business career you'll encounter them all. Where should you start reading, then? Here are some brief summaries to help you decide.

The Pitfalls of Parenting Mature Companies

The first case in the collection, by John Strahinich, takes a jab at a mainstay of strategy theory—Bruce Henderson's famous "growth share matrix" for setting investment priorities. The matrix focuses diversified companies on their rising stars, based on market growth rate and market share, and counters a common tendency to overinvest in mature businesses. These "cash cows," it says, should be milked for funds to invest in business units with better growth potential. But what if you're the manager herding one of those "cows"? In this case, Charlie Crescent is in that position, and he isn't content to see his division ride slowly into the sunset. He sees opportunities for innovation, and wants to plow some of the division's ample profits back into its own business. This puts Charlie's bosses in a dilemma. He's a great performer, but as his unwillingness to follow current strategy mounts, should they simply replace him? Perhaps another manager would be easier to keep down on the farm.

Most of the commentators on the case see the problem not as a clash of managerial ambitions, but as a more basic failure of growth strategy. Michael Goold of Ashridge Strategic Management Centre simply rejects what he calls "the portfolio management game." Management, he says, should think about the intrinsic merits of the company's different businesses and figure out how to add the most value to each of them. Orit Gadiesh of Bain & Company stops short of condemning portfolio management, but stresses that the case company, Sargon Corporation, must be more clear whether its intent is to be a pure portfolio company or a "value-added parent" that makes the whole greater than the sum of its parts. Harvard Business School's David Collis agrees with Goold that the whole notion of cash cows funding emerging businesses is wrongheaded. He points out that the capital markets are the most efficient allocators of capital; each of Sargon's businesses should have a sufficiently credible strategy that the corporation can raise the necessary finances on its behalf. As Sargon management works to clarify its strategic plan, Jane Warner, president of Randall Textron, suggests it may want to bring in some outside resources. Given how long the current team has worked together, the issues may be clouded by old patterns of interaction.

Go Global—or No?

Walter Kuemmerle's case study brings up two sets of issues: strategy formulation around foreign markets, and the extent to which a first-mover must overextend itself to scale up fast and fend off fast-following competition. The company involved, DataClear, is young, and its basic software could be developed and marketed in any number of directions. The big decision facing its CEO, Greg McNally, is whether to focus on creating new applications for other industries domestically, or on going global with its current core product. Or must it do both at once? An emerging competitor on the European scene seems to turn up the heat on the question.

Only the first of the four commentators is gung ho on the prospect of going global. Heather Killen, senior vice president of international operations at Yahoo!, says that remaining a domestic U.S. player is simply not an option. DataClear is right to be considering alliances as the way to gain a foothold, but instead of joint venturing with a small niche player, it should find a partner with the scale of an SAP. But BCG's Alison Sander urges the CEO to consider other options like licensing the software, selling it on the Web, or hiring local sales representatives. Both she and the third commentator, venture capitalist Barry Schiffman, advise McNally to keep the company on its current course, building close relationships in domestic markets with companies that will give it global access over time. For Schiffman, the issue is one of insufficient managerial experience and capital to expand more aggressively. Scott Schnell's commentary strikes the balance. Head of marketing at a Massachusetts-based software company, Schnell concedes that DataClear will have to expand internationally at some point, but believes the challenge is not so immediate as to cause panic. McNally should take a few months to personally lead the formulation of a strategy, and meanwhile remember that businesses win by building from a strong, defensible market position with a top-performing product and supporting organizational infrastructure.

Stick to the Core—or Go for More?

When a business is doing one thing extremely well— as in an advertising firm that does terrific creative work—should it stick to its knitting, and grow by finding more customers to buy that one thing? Or should it move beyond that core competence and find ways to serve more of its loyal customers' needs? That's the essential strategic dilemma addressed in this case by Tom Waite. The two cofounders and leading talents of advertising agency Advaark are in disagreement about the way forward, after one opportunistic foray into a new area, product strategy consulting, proves successful. George Caldwell reminds his partner that "when we formed this business, we agreed that the key to our long-term success was staying focused on what we do best—creating unforgettable ads." But Ian Rafferty counters with his own logic: Doing more business with existing clients would reduce the overall cost of sales. "We know we want to grow, and here we have a client begging us to provide it with a new service. Why on earth wouldn't we do that?"

The commentators' answers to that question are, naturally, divided. John Whitney of Columbia Business School reminds us that "the corporate junk pile is littered with companies that overlooked risks to their core business while pursuing new opportunities." He tells Advaark to keep its focus on ad making. The opposite advice is given by Roland Rust of the University of Maryland. An outspoken advocate of pursuing "customer equity," Rust says Advaark's goal should be to increase the lifetime value of its customers. Rafferty, he says, "should be given free rein to bring Advaark's business into line with what customers are saying they want." Gordon McCallum, in charge of group strategy at Virgin, agrees—but for different reasons. This is not simply a strategic issue, he says, but an organizational one. The greatest danger is that the crack team of Caldwell and Rafferty will split up over the disagreement. Why not let Rafferty give it a try, in a limited, low-risk way? In the end, strategic elegance is less important than talent. At Virgin, McCallum says, "we have found that the abilities of the people leading the organization determine whether we end up with a pig or a pony." In a final commentary, Chris Zook, a director at Bain & Company—who can be expected, as author of *Profit from the Core*, to advise a tight strategic focus—throws us an interesting hook by damning not only Advaark's potential wanderings from its core, but also those of its client, GlobalBev. Zook outlines the five steps that he takes consulting clients through to evaluate strategic growth initiatives.

Growing for Broke

Some businesspeople are fond of citing a fact about sharks—that they must constantly move forward (with their mouths open, no less) to survive. It seems a handy metaphor for the so-called "growth imperative"—that a business must continue to grow, organically or by gobbling up others, to avoid lapsing into a downward spiral. But is growth for its own sake really sound strategy? That's the question posed by this case by Paul Hemp. Written in the first person, it reveals the mindset of its CEO protagonist, a Greek immigrant to America named Nicky Anaptyxi, as he contemplates a major acquisition. His Paragon Tool has been growing fast, and the business Nicky is targeting next, MonitoRobotics, could yield not only more revenue, but the beginnings of a shift from product supplier to solutions provider. But chief financial officer (CFO) William Littlefield isn't so enamored of the deal. To his way of thinking, it's time for Paragon to take a break from its feeding frenzy and focus on bottom-line profitability.

The first piece of advice from the commentators is a bit surprising, considering its source. Rand Araskog famously pared down ITT after his predecessor Harold Geneen had built it up into a sprawling conglomerate.

But he says Nicky should follow his instincts and make the acquisition—first, because they may be right, and second, because they are his instincts. He's the one who has to have the greatest faith in any strategy, if it's to be well executed. Ken Favaro, on the other hand, plays to type in his commentary. As head of Marakon Associates, a consultancy that helps clients focus relentlessly on value creation, he notes that there isn't enough evidence to suggest that the acquisition will prove profitable within three years—a common objective of venture capitalists that should be adopted by managers. But Brian Arthur of the Santa Fe Institute says the acquisition is "an obvious go." For him, the case is more about repositioning than growth, and he believes the new positioning has enough potential to justify the temporary losses it will create. Finally, Jay Gellert, CEO of Health Net, gives the advice that Rand Araskog didn't. Having presided over a turnaround in which his company divested itself of several disappointing acquisitions, he wants to see more rigor in Nicky's analysis. He also worries that CFO Littlefield might resign over a deal he doesn't support—which would "set off alarm bells" on Wall Street.

Cross Selling or Cross Purposes?

Sales management consultant Ford Harding created his case to throw light on a common stumbling block in companies' growth strategies: the failure of their customer-facing people to "cross sell" offerings from other divisions of the same company. At TopTek, it's the people selling "product"—the company's software packages—and the people selling consulting who aren't pitching each other's wares. CEO John Vaunt suspects the problem—and the way to fix it—is with the company's compensation system. If only he can make it in everyone's selfish financial interests to represent a broader range of the company's offerings, then the synergies TopTek expects will materialize. But various clues in the story suggest there's more to the issue than incentives.

Corporate governance expert Ram Charan is the first commentator to criticize John Vaunt for his blind spot. Vaunt, Charan says, is "falling into the trap that catches so many CEOs when they are too hands-off—looking to the compensation system to get the job done." TopTek would be better off spending its resources to train its salespeople along lines that Charan describes. Caroline Kovac, general manager of IBM Healthcare and Life Sciences, thinks an even deeper cultural transformation needs to occur. She makes an interesting distinction between salespeople who are hunters, always chasing down new deals, and salespeople who are farmers, cultivating relationships to be harvested over the long term. TopTek's people have to align around its new mission of selling solutions. Sales compensation specialist Jerry Colletti offers plenty of very useful advice on how John Vaunt might want to design TopTek's incentives to promote the behaviors he's seeking—but he urges him to address some more fundamental issues first. The last word goes to Federico Turegano, who has lived the issues raised by the case in his leadership role at Société Générale's investment banking group. His pragmatic take? That "TopTek management needs to manage the tension between these camps but at the same time recognize that some friction is inevitable—and not necessarily a bad thing."

A Rose by Any Other Name

The last case of the collection, by Dan Stone, covers strategic territory familiar to anyone in the consumer goods industry—the shift of channel power from manufacturers to retailers, and specifically the rise of private-label merchandise. It's the story of Rose Partyware, and it begins as the company's leadership finds itself at a crossroads. On the one hand, it has an ambitious and capable new marketing director urging management to fund a splashy new branding campaign. On the other, it has a huge retail customer hoping to contract its services for strictly behind-the-scenes work—as the manufacturer of a new private-label line the retailer wants to put on its shelves. The margins on the private-label work are, of course, slimmer than what Rose is used to, and the risk of cannibalizing its own sales of branded merchandise in those stores is obvious. But if it doesn't take the job, the retailer will only give it to a competitor, leaving Rose with the same lost sales and no revenues to help make up for them.

The first perspective on the case comes from Frank Weise, the chairman, president, and CEO of private-label soft drink producer Cott. Naturally, he believes Rose should accept its retail customer's offer and actively partner with it around product development. The best way to do that while also serving Rose's own brand, he explains, is to ask the retailer to let Rose manage the entire category in its stores. But Reebok's chief marketing officer, Mickey Pant, advises the opposite strategy. As risky as it is, a brand-building campaign will position Rose much better for future profitability. Not to put too fine a point on it, "Rose will be shooting itself in the foot" if it helps build the retailer's brand, although it may make some money in the short run. Stephen Hoch of the Wharton School of Business lands somewhere in between, advising Rose to move into the private-label business—even while admitting that it doesn't make sense for most national brand manufacturers. The key, in Hoch's opinion, is that whichever way Rose goes, it cannot compromise its quality. Judith and Marcel Corstjens, authors of the book *Store Wars*, write an equally nuanced commentary, but land on the other side of the balance. But part of their reasoning sets aside the logic of the strategy per se, and emphasizes the importance of how much real commitment is behind it. Rose's management, as the

Corstjenses perceive it, will bring more spirit to the cause of building its own brand.

Getting Somewhere

In the final commentary to the final case in this collection is a notion that might, to some readers, seem to undermine the whole volume. "We often see organizations get fixated on choosing the one best strategy," write Judith and Marcel Corstjens. "There is often no one superior strategy; several might lead to a sustainable advantage. Just as important is the will behind it." It's not an isolated thought; in a business world currently smitten with "execution," (that, for instance, was the title of Larry Bossidy's and Ram Charan's recent blockbuster business book), we hear variants of it every day.

But for most businesses most of the time, having the right strategy matters very much indeed. Since strategic decisions are made infrequently, and their repercussions are vast, they deserve extraordinary deliberation. Again, we can look to Lewis Carroll for insight. Recall where we left Alice, not knowing where she wanted to go, and being told by the Cheshire Cat that, in that case, it didn't matter which way she went. "—so long as I get somewhere," Alice added as an explanation. "Oh, you're sure to do that," said the Cat, "if you only walk long enough."

Few of us in today's business environment have the luxury of that long walk. Read these cases, formulate your own opinion, and compare notes with the expert commentators, and you'll become a more practiced strategic thinker. Down the road, that just might save you a few steps.

JOHN STRAHINICH

The Pitfalls of Parenting

Mature Companies

Executive Summary

Jack Marlowe, Sargon Corporation's president, is wrestling with one of the most intractable problems he has dealt with since joining the company: what to do about Arcell, Sargon's mature household-appliances unit, and Charlie Crescent, its president.

CEO Hal Hestnes and Marlowe are forging a new identity for Sargon—formerly a small defense contractor—as a diversified manufacturer. The company's businesses now include brake systems, components for telecommunications equipment, and voice recognition systems, and Sargon has recently acquired a manufacturer of routers and hubs for corporate networks. But Wall Street is taking a dim view of Sargon's strategy. It seems to think that Sargon is stretching itself too thin.

That's where Arcell comes in. Sargon is counting on the unit to provide the lion's share of the money for the company's investment in its future. Marlowe has made it clear to Crescent that he expects Arcell to run lean and mean. And Crescent has said that he understands. But his actions don't show it. He keeps wanting to plow his profits back into Arcell.

Marlowe faces several questions: Should he replace Crescent? If so, where should he put this valued employee? Wouldn't whoever replaced Crescent be equally frustrated at having to lead a unit that the company considers a cash cow?

Four experts analyze Marlowe's problem in this fictitious case study: Michael Goold, a specialist in corporate strategy; Orit Gadiesh, chairman of a strategy consulting firm; David J. Collis, a business professor; and Jane Warner, president of a diversified manufacturing company.

"Remember, Jack," said Hal Hestnes, "swords into plowshares."

"And guns to butter," said Jack Marlowe, managing a weak smile for the old man's benefit as he started down the hall back to his office.

The "swords into plowshares" routine had begun as an inside joke between the two men—an allusion to a tough but fairly accurate profile of their company, Sargon Corporation, that had appeared several years earlier in a national monthly magazine. The writer had used the two phrases to describe chairman and CEO Hestnes's strategy. Without losing any of its humor, the routine had become something of a mantra for Hestnes and for Marlowe, the 49-year-old president of Sargon. Their plan was to forge a new identity for Sargon— once a small defense contractor and now primarily an appliance company—as a diversified manufacturer poised to take advantage of the new and growing economies in the global marketplace.

For the moment, however, all humor was lost on Marlowe as he wrestled with one of the most intractable problems he had dealt with since joining

Sargon as a young, freshly minted business-school graduate. What to do about Arcell Corporation, Sargon's household-appliances unit? And, for that matter, what to do about Charlie Crescent, Arcell's president?

Marlowe replayed the conversation he had just had with Hestnes over lunch. "We've been talking this to death for weeks, Jack," Hestnes had said. "Do we let Crescent go? Do we keep him but rein in his plans for Arcell? Move him to another unit? Or, if the answer is D—none of the above—what in blazes *do* we do?"

Marlowe checked his watch as he banked left past the neat rows of desks that led to his office. It was just past 1 P.M.—less than five hours until he and Hestnes were scheduled to leave for a white-tie charity fundraiser. "I'll want to hear more of your thoughts about this on the way into town," Hestnes had said. Marlowe suspected that meant he had better show up with a solution.

Marlowe motioned Steff Ferris, his assistant, into his office and asked her to cancel his afternoon appointments and hold all his calls.

"Does that include Chris Freed's 4 o'clock?" Ferris asked, referring to Sargon's chief of R&D. "She really needs to go over her budget proposal with you."

"If she can keep it to under ten minutes, fine," Marlowe said. "Otherwise, it's going to have to wait until tomorrow."

"I'll tell her," Ferris said.

Marlowe sat down at his desk and turned his attention to the yellow legal pad that he had pulled from his drawer. His thinking pad, Ferris called it. He had already covered about half a page with sprawling notes when she drifted quietly out of his office.

All right, Marlowe told himself as he began to outline the issues. The first thing to do is to drain the emotion from the situation.

That meant ignoring any resentment he harbored toward the old man for framing the problem so starkly. *Old man.* Hestnes was only 11 years his senior, but the time he had spent at the helm of Sargon had taken its toll, reminding Marlowe of those before-and-after pictures of U.S. presidents. Hestnes was right, of course. They *had* been chewing the issue to death for weeks.

Look at it from Hestnes's point of view, thought Marlowe. Sargon's nondefense businesses included everything from household appliances (which Hestnes's predecessor had gotten them into in the early 1970s) to brake systems for the automotive industry (which had always been a sideline at Sargon) to components for telecommunications equipment (a business that Hestnes had launched in 1983) to voice recognition systems for the security industry (a 1989 acquisition). By the end of the year, those businesses were expected to account for half of Sargon's profits. That was a far cry from 1977, when Hestnes had taken over and the company's defense business was delivering practically all of Sargon's earnings. So much for the good news.

The bad news was that Wall Street seemed to be taking a dim view of Hestnes's strategy. That despite a vigorous cash flow, little debt, and the company's current program to buy back shares. The pros just didn't seem to be accepting Sargon's new identity. The company's recent acquisition of Cyberam, a maker of routers and hubs for corporate networks, had met with virtually no applause outside Sargon headquarters. Cyberam had a good deal of potential but negligible market share. It was also a bit of a stretch for Sargon—just beyond the company's current manufacturing capabilities—and the press and Wall Street had expressed doubts about Hestnes's ability to make the move succeed.

But that's where Arcell was supposed to come in. Sargon's shrinking defense business was still providing some cash for the parent company's investment in its future, but Sargon was now counting on Arcell to provide the lion's share of the money. From day one, that's how Hestnes had seen Arcell's role in the company. And when Charlie Crescent had taken over the appliances unit two years earlier, the first thing he had done—with Hestnes's full blessing—was to launch a major consolidation and cost-cutting effort. In those two years, he had lifted Arcell's operating margin from 2% to 7%.

The trouble was, Crescent didn't always seem to get the big picture at Sargon. His insistence on quality was laudable, and he was taking an active part in the company's best-practices and conversion-technology programs. In fact, he was working closely with Chris Freed on a project to adapt the heat-resistant material used on Sargon's missiles to the tops of Arcell's stoves. At the same time, though, Crescent was making endless requests to plow his profits back into his group for new, state-of-the-art machinery, for an updated computer system for his purchasing department, for establishing a sales force in China—for this, that, and the other thing. Marlowe thought he had made it clear to Crescent from the start that Sargon was counting on Arcell to run lean and mean. And Crescent had said that he understood. But his actions just didn't show it.

What was worse, every time Marlowe turned down his requests, Crescent seemed to grow increasingly alienated. His resentment sometimes bordered on hostility and outright insubordination. He had made no effort, for instance, to disguise what he thought of

---

"I can't keep my people motivated if you won't let us live up to our potential."

Sargon's acquisition of Cyberam. Marlowe remembered the conversation clearly. Crescent had been on the phone to Marlowe within minutes of receiving the internal announcement.

"You guys back East are having so much fun running with the bulls," Crescent had cracked, "it's no wonder you think of us here in the heartland as Elsie, the cash cow. But I'll tell you, I don't think this is a good move. You can't continue to count on us as your safety net unless you give us what we need to grow. You're forcing us to stagnate, Jack. I can't keep my people motivated if you won't let us live up to our potential."

Marlowe had calmed him down, temporarily, by saying that he thought Crescent's proposals for increased R&D funding and for a greater investment in building a dealer network had merit, and by assuring him that he was considering them seriously. But he also had the feeling that his reassurances had fallen flat. Marlowe himself was only lukewarm about Crescent's ideas, and he knew that Hestnes wouldn't approve. Crescent probably suspected as much. His political survival skills had kicked in during the phone call—he hadn't exploded—but he had probably started swearing as soon as he hung up.

Marlowe smiled in spite of himself. Crescent had always been outspoken. It was one of the traits that Marlowe admired in him. The two men went back a long way. Years ago, Marlowe had been dispatched on a troubleshooting assignment to Arcell's Indiana headquarters. Crescent was then the company's youngest plant superintendent, and the two men had struck up a fast friendship. Crescent seemed to know every nook, every job, and every person at Arcell. He should, he joked; half of the employees were his relatives. But Marlowe knew better. Crescent was a natural leader.

"The more you lead," Crescent would say with a wink, "the less you have to manage."

Marlowe needed to take a walk. As he left his office, his eyes were fixed in a 1,000-yard stare, which he had come by honestly in Vietnam and had cultivated since then to discourage small talk in passersby. In the men's room, he splashed cold water on his face. On his way back into his office, he noticed Ferris on the line. Cupping the receiver, she mouthed Chris Freed's name.

"Patch her through to me," Marlowe said.

Back inside his office, Marlowe picked up his phone. "Chris, sorry for standing you up this afternoon," he said.

"No problem," said Freed. "Steff said you were up against it. She penciled me in for tomorrow morning."

Marlowe appreciated Freed's patience. He also respected her judgment. He decided to solicit her opinion, albeit obliquely, on Crescent.

"How's the Arcell project going?" Marlowe asked.

"Fine," said Freed, not taking the bait. "We can discuss it tomorrow."

"No, really," Marlowe said. "I want to hear about it now. Give me the broad brush strokes."

Freed told him about the coating process her lab had come up with to spray the missile material on Arcell's stove tops. "It's only about 5% cheaper than our current process," she said apologetically, "and we haven't seen as much of an improvement in durability as we had hoped. But frankly, I think it's the best we can do."

"Hmm," said Marlowe. "What's Charlie say?"

Freed hesitated. Marlowe repeated the question.

"Charlie's balking," Freed finally said. "He wants us to spend more time on research. Originally, we thought we could reduce costs by 10%." Freed spoke the next few sentences slowly. "Charlie also seems to believe that customers will think we've lowered our standards. The focus groups haven't reacted well to the look of the new surface, and Charlie thinks that if we go ahead with it, consumers will interpret it as a cost-cutting move without any benefit. He really thought he would be sitting on a revolutionized stove top. And maybe we could be. But this was intended as a cost-cutting project and as a way to take our expertise from one part of the company and use it throughout. The problem is, we're out of time and money at this end. We can't keep playing at this forever. We're behind the curve already on our project for the telecommunications unit."

"Why didn't you tell me this sooner?" Marlowe said, barely concealing his annoyance.

"You've been under the gun yourself lately," said Freed, "so I figured it would keep until our budget session. But to be perfectly honest, Jack, if Charlie doesn't decide to roll out the new stove top now, I'd just as soon scrap the whole project and save the bucks."

Marlowe finished up the conversation, promising more time to discuss the issue in the morning, and then returned to the questions at hand: what to do about Crescent and Arcell. Marlowe knew that Hestnes already had a replacement in mind—Pat Jameson, second-in-command in telecommunications. Jameson had championed the Cyberam acquisition and had done most of the legwork required to bring the company into the Sargon family with as little upheaval as possible. She was capable, but Marlowe wasn't certain that she had the temperament and the patience to run a mature business like major appliances. Besides, Crescent was still widely respected by his people, even though he had led the company's painful downsizing. Replacing him could put Jameson in a tough spot.

And who was to say that Jameson wouldn't act the same as Crescent, given Arcell's position? Crescent had an ego—that was certain. But still, it had to be hard for him to sit during Sargon strategy meetings and listen for two hours to plans for growing Cyberam *and* plans for growing the voice-recognition-systems division *and* plans for growing the telecommunications business. Crescent usually got the floor for about ten minutes at those meetings—just enough time for Hestnes to hear that Arcell was performing as expected. Crescent always left looking disgruntled. Wouldn't Jameson become just as frustrated? How was Sargon supposed to motivate the leader—any leader—of a company that wasn't expected to grow?

And where to put Crescent if they did replace him? He was too valuable to let go. Maybe the thing to do was to try to pacify Hestnes—and sit tight for a few months.

"Less is more, Hal," Marlowe said out loud.

After all, Arcell was nicely positioned to grab its share of the market—and more—when China and Eastern Europe opened up, he thought. Crescent has a plan to expand, and he has an organization that he must manage—people he needs to motivate. It wasn't at all like the shrinking defense business, in which the division head had been close to retirement and not at all interested in pushing the company to go on. Employees had moved into Sargon's new businesses— or out of the company—fairly smoothly. But would China and Eastern Europe ever open up the way Crescent envisioned? And could Sargon afford to back Crescent's plans and give adequate support to the organization's critical growth businesses as well? Cyberam needed hand-holding. The voice-recognition-systems division was still sharing space and administrative personnel with one of the telecommunications units, and it needed steady investment to grow and to secure its niche. And Hal Hestnes was not the kind of guy you advised to stand pat and do nothing.

Ferris knocked at his door and poked her head in. "It's 5:45—you'd better get ready," she said. "If you don't need me anymore, I'd like to take off."

"Thanks for minding the gate," Marlowe said. When she had closed the door behind her, Marlowe slipped into his tux, grabbed his overcoat and brief-case, and headed for the front door of the building. The car had already pulled up, and Hestnes was waiting in the backseat. Marlowe got in and pulled the door shut behind him.

"Take your time," Hestnes told the driver as he raised the inside window for privacy. "Mr. Marlowe here has something to tell me."

What Advice Should Marlowe Give the CEO?

Four experts discuss how to manage mature businesses.

➤ Michael Goold

Michael Goold is a director of the Ashridge Strategic Management Centre, a research, teaching, and consulting organization based in London. His research focuses on corporate strategy and the management of multibusiness companies. Goold is the author of Corporate-Level Strategy: Creating Value in the Multibusiness Company *(John Wiley & Sons, 1994) and* Strategies and Styles *(Basil Blackwell, 1987).*

As Sargon's president, Jack Marlowe is responsible for implementing the company's corporate-level strategy. Under this strategy, the role of Arcell Corporation, the mature household-appliances business, is to provide cash so that Sargon can reinvest in newer, more rapidly growing businesses such as Cyberam. But Marlowe is also aware that by squeezing as much cash as possible out of Arcell, he may well be holding back the division's development and frustrating the competent and successful management team headed by Charlie Crescent. Corporate parents that treat their mature businesses as cash cows to be milked in order to pay for more glamorous investments elsewhere in the portfolio inevitably create such conflicts and resentments.

Resolving Marlowe's dilemma is not difficult. He needs to stop playing the balanced-portfolio game. That is, he should stop expecting all of Sargon's mature businesses to

---

Sargon may have pushed its diversification program too far away from its mature businesses.

---

act simply as cash generators and all of its new businesses to grow quickly and soak up the cash thrown off by the mature businesses. Instead, he should think about the intrinsic merits of the company's different businesses and try to figure out how Sargon, as a corporate parent, can add the most value to each of them.

Let's start with Arcell. The business's recent performance is impressive. It's no surprise that Crescent is getting more ambitious and asking for investments in new products, new facilities, and new markets. The critical judgment call for Marlowe and CEO Hal Hestnes is to decide whether they think those investment proposals are sound. If they do, they should give Crescent as much encouragement and support as possible. If they don't, they should rein in his ambitions and scale back his plans. The decision should turn on the merits of the Arcell proposals, not on the needs of Cyberam or any of the other businesses. Otherwise, the corporate parent may well end up destroying value rather than adding it.

Now consider Sargon's growth businesses. The parent company has diversified extensively in order to move away from the defense sector. Granted, it has stayed within the very broad realm of manufacturing. But I doubt whether Sargon has the competencies it needs to manage its newer businesses successfully. Slogans like Swords into Plowshares sound fine, but they often disguise a lack of rigorous thinking about what sorts of businesses a company can manage well and add value to. I suspect that Hestnes and Marlowe have pushed Sargon's diversification program too far away from their mature "heartland" businesses. They are unlikely to have a good feel for what it takes to succeed in businesses as different as defense, household appliances, telecommunications components, and voice recognition systems. If so, further investments in those diversifications are unlikely to pay off. Wall Street has probably spotted the problem already; that may be why it is taking a "dim view" of Hestnes's strategy.

What should Marlowe do? First, without worrying too much about the other businesses in Sargon's portfolio, he should figure out how he can help Arcell improve its performance. For mature businesses, the role of the corporate parent is often to ensure that a suitably lean and mean approach is taken and to weed out overambitious plans for growth or diversification. If Marlowe decides that Crescent is being overly optimistic about what can be achieved, he should explain clearly to the Arcell management team why they will not be getting the funding they want. And if, at the extreme, he concludes that Crescent is completely out of touch with the realities of his business, he may decide that another, tougher manager is needed to run Arcell.

On the other hand, if Marlowe concludes that Crescent has identified some genuinely worthwhile opportunities, he should do whatever he can to help the company succeed. That may mean providing additional investment, technical help, or other kinds of support. In such a situation, the corporate parent can add the most value by making skills and resources available—either from other parts of the corporation or from outside—to help the mature business accomplish its goals. In any case, Marlowe should make clear that, in principle, he is fully willing to support investments in Arcell that he believes will earn a good return for Sargon's shareholders.

Right now, Marlowe is probably unsure about the quality of Arcell's investment proposals. If so, he needs to spend more time with the business in order to form an opinion. He should make plans to sit down with Crescent and the other Arcell managers and go through their ideas carefully enough to form his own independent judgment of their worth. Good corporate parents of mature businesses are distinguished by their understanding of the real opportunities and pitfalls that face the businesses, not by their willingness to make snap judgments in accordance with some theoretical notion of a balanced portfolio.

This leads me to Marlowe's second challenge. He must persuade Hestnes to reconsider Sargon's corporate-level strategy. What sorts of businesses does it really make sense for Sargon to own? What skills and resources does the corporate team have, and in what businesses can they be used most effectively? How can Sargon get the most out of its mature businesses? Is it really in the shareholders'—or any other stakeholders'—interests to diversify so widely? What kinds of growth and financing goals are realistic and achievable?

It will take more than a car journey to reach agreement on those issues. And Hestnes may not be too happy when he hears that Marlowe doesn't have a quick-fix solution to the current dilemma. But until the larger strategic issues are resolved, Sargon will continue to have problems with businesses like Arcell and managers like Crescent. And despite everyone's hard work, the organization will continue to falter.

➤ Orit Gadiesh

Orit Gadiesh is chairman of the board of Bain & Company, an international strategy consulting firm based in Boston, Massachusetts.

Jack Marlowe should hope that it's a long ride. He and Hestnes have at least five critical strategic questions they must begin addressing together. What they do about Charlie Crescent will depend on the answers, which they probably should have agreed on long ago. Let me phrase the questions as Marlowe might put them to Sargon's CEO:

As the parent company, what's our mission? Is Sargon to be a pure portfolio company, whose primary purpose is generating cash by buying and selling businesses? In that case, Hestnes and Marlowe necessarily will act as financial managers, keeping themselves removed, for the most part, from managerial issues at the divisions. Or do they want Sargon to be what I call a *value-added parent*, making the whole greater than the sum of its parts by managing the organization's core competencies and creating synergies among its various divisions? Wall Street's lukewarm response to the company may reflect the fact that the analysts have picked up on its leaders' confusion.

Unfortunately, Hestnes and Marlowe's stated mission—"to forge a new identity for Sargon as a diversified manufacturer poised to take advantage of the new and growing economies in the global marketplace"—doesn't make clear what kind of company they want Sargon to be. Nor do their actions. On the one hand, they want to buy new businesses and grow them. On the other, they've been trying to share people and expertise across divisions. The reality, however, is that they won't be able to do either effectively unless they are clear about their strategic intent.

The Cyberam acquisition shows where a lack of clarity can lead. Cyberam doesn't seem to be a global company, and it has no appreciable market share, so it appears an unlikely candidate for building up and selling off under a portfolio strategy. But neither does it seem to draw on or extend Sargon's core competencies. How can it add value to the company's other divisions? What's more, one would think that if Hestnes and Marlowe wanted to share expertise across the company, they would include senior managers from the different divisions in their decisions about acquisitions. They certainly didn't ask Crescent for his opinion before acquiring Cyberam.

What are our specific goals for Sargon? Have Hestnes and Marlowe thought through where they want the company to be in a year? Five years? Ten? Is it possible that the CEO is concentrating on growth but not paying enough attention to ensuring that that growth ends up being profitable?

Too many companies grow very fast but never achieve profitability. Bain recently looked at 1,500 companies with more than $1 billion in revenues and found that less than 10% were able to grow at an annual rate of 8% and still earn their cost of capital over time. If Hestnes and Marlowe are to avoid this trap, they need to understand the dynamics of their business. They must think through the underlying economics of each industry they are in and envision how they intend to make Sargon a player—the number one or two company—in each. If they focus on profitable growth, they can better understand the trade-offs involved and the short- and long-term implications of each move they make.

So how do we achieve profitable growth? Does Hestnes foresee Sargon continuing to grow solely by acquisition? Or does he want it also to grow organically—that is, by expanding the businesses or the expertise it already owns? In my experience, the most successful growth companies are those that build organically on their base of core customers or core competencies.

As a rule, companies that grow organically have these qualities:

- Their senior managers genuinely seek change. Hestnes and Marlowe seem unsure of where they stand on this front.

- All the members of the top management team share a common, consistent view of the future. Marlowe and Hestnes clearly are not on the same wavelength. Crescent is butting heads with both of them. There's no consistency here.

- Their managers are willing to take considered risks to get to where they want to go. In the process of investing, they develop a carefully thought through rationale for each investment decision. If the rationales are consistent over time, others in the organization will understand how to think through decisions on possible investment for themselves. Here Hestnes and Marlowe don't seem to have a rationale for explaining to Crescent why his ideas for investment don't make sense (if indeed they believe that they don't).

- They are always watching the competition and have a strong focus on the customer. They know the value of market share and market leadership. Hestnes and Marlowe keep getting their company into businesses with different sets of customers and different competitors, which doesn't make focusing on either any easier. At the same time, they are ignoring the fact that those new businesses are not market leaders. To his credit, Crescent seems to understand his customers' likes and dislikes, which leads me to think that he probably also has a good sense of Arcell's potential in the industry. He also seems to have a fast, flexible organization ready to roll out a revised strategy the minute he gets the nod from Hestnes. But Crescent may be alone in his class. Which brings me to the next question.

How exactly should we at Sargon, the parent, be managing our different businesses to achieve our overall corporate goals? In this context, Hestnes and Marlowe should think hard about the definition and proper use of a cash cow. Do they want to drain Arcell quickly or invest in it and milk it over time? They seem to be doing the former, but if they decide to treat the division as a cash cow, I would hold that the latter is the better strategic option. Sargon's new businesses are likely to require cash for a long time.

On the other hand, even if management does decide that Arcell is a mature business, why can't a mature business still be an engine, or a platform, for growth? Hestnes and Marlowe might consider letting Crescent continue to build Arcell's business by extending what it offers to its core customers. USAA is a good example of a company that pursues such a strategy; it has consistently broadened the range of services it provides to its existing customers. Or they might want to steer Arcell to gain market share by focusing on a core competence. For example, it could strengthen its position as a low-cost producer, perhaps by making related acquisitions around the world, much as Emerson Electric has done.

The point is that Hestnes and Marlowe must understand the distinctive factors that drive each of Sargon's businesses. How can each division achieve maximum performance? How can corporate help those efforts along?

But again, as a prerequisite to everything else, Hestnes and Marlowe must figure out what kind of company they want theirs to be—a portfolio company or an integrated whole. Then they can determine how each division's needs fit with the overall corporate strategy. They should communicate their understanding to the division heads—indeed, to all of Sargon's managers. With a better understanding of the parent organization's objectives, this larger group will have a better sense of how to manage, what to manage, and how much to manage. The company's board of directors might be interested as well.

What kind of people do we need to enable Sargon to succeed in its mission? Are Hestnes and Marlowe being sufficiently thoughtful in making executive staffing decisions? I doubt it. They seem to be entertaining a lot of options on the fly and not trying that hard to match people to the task at hand. It takes a completely different kind of person to manage a company for growth than to manage it for cash. What makes them think Pat Jameson will be able to lead Arcell?

And why are they so frustrated with Crescent? Here they have someone who has done everything they want him to do. He led his unit through a painful downsizing and cost-cutting process, and his employees still love him. He needs only ten minutes to present his reports at senior management meetings because he always hits his numbers. He understands his customers, he is eager to leverage expertise from other units, and he is champing at the bit to produce even more than he currently is. He is not afraid to give feedback to his bosses, which may be a bit threatening to Hestnes and Marlowe but is, in fact, an *extremely* valuable quality.

To me, he looks like a terrific manager; I wouldn't even consider letting him go. If they want to drain Arcell as quickly as possible, then he probably isn't the right person to head the division. But if they have growth opportunities in another division, he looks like a good guy to put at the helm.

In sum, Crescent is a manager who seems to be asking for logical, smart things. Hestnes said early on that he wasn't going to focus on Arcell—but that was before it started doing so well. Reevaluate it, guys.

Of course, it would help to know Sargon's financials, its market shares, and the size of its investments. But even without those numbers, we can see that the company's CEO and president really should step back, answer some fundamental strategic questions, and consider the situation at hand from the broad, balanced perspective that having the answers to the questions will provide. If they don't, Crescent will quit, Arcell will flounder, and Hestnes and Marlowe may find themselves sitting in the middle of a corporate ruin instead of presiding over a whole that at least has promise.

➤ David J. Collis

David J. Collis is an associate professor at the Harvard Business School in Boston, Massachusetts. He is coauthor, with Cynthia Montgomery, of Corporate Strategy: Resources and the Scope of the Firm *(Richard D. Irwin, 1996).*

If Jack Marlowe is truly focusing his attention on Charlie Crescent, he is missing the point—and possibly putting Sargon in jeopardy. Nothing can be decided about Crescent until Sargon's overall corporate strategy has been reevaluated.

Sargon's senior managers appear to be making two fundamental mistakes with regard to corporate strategy. First, they are holding on to the misguided belief that value can be created in a corporate portfolio by transferring capital from one business to another. The traditional approach of portfolio planning, which was widely practiced in the 1970s, was to take funds from cash-cow businesses and invest them in high-growth, emerging businesses that would then become the stars of the corporation. If there is any lesson for diversified companies to take away from the 1980s, however, it is that the *capital markets* are the most efficient allocators of capital. Although it is true that raising capital (particularly new equity) may be more expensive than retaining earnings, any business strategy that is viable should enable a company to raise the capital it requires. Sargon should not be using Arcell as a cash cow to fund its new businesses; each business should have a sufficiently credible strategy that the corporation can raise the necessary finances on its behalf.

The second corporate-strategy mistake Sargon's managers appear to be making has to do with the company's diversification plans. The Cyberam acquisition, whose announcement received such a cool reception on Wall Street, seems to be only the most extreme example of the weakness in the strategy. What do household appliances, brake systems, telecommunications components, voice recognition systems, and routers have in common? Other than that they are nondefense and high technology, and have great growth potential, they seem to share nothing—no technology, no manufacturing processes, no customers.

The diversification strategy appears to be a mad dash to get into any nondefense business that might even remotely be claimed to have a synergy with the company's defense activities. The problem that Arcell is having finding a worthwhile use for the missile coating is typical of the difficulty many companies have creating economic value by competing in both defense and nondefense businesses.

Marlowe, therefore, has a lot of work to do before he can resolve the alleged problem with Crescent. First, he needs to reassess the corporation's strategy. If he does not believe in the strategy, he should confront Hestnes. If, for some strange reason, the diversification plans do make sense to Marlowe, he still should use his analysis of the strategy to convince Hestnes that funding acquisitions with Arcell's cash is inappropriate.

In either case, once Marlowe has established that the strategy for Arcell must be separated from the diversification move, he should begin to think about what, in fact, is best for Arcell—independent of the arbitrary corporate mandate to generate cash. It is unclear whether Arcell should or should not be investing in itself. Is there a real future in China? Will investment in a dealer network pay off? Such questions must be answered before Marlowe can know whether or not Crescent is the right manager. Only if it turns out that Arcell really should be managed as a no-growth, low-cost operation does Marlowe have a potential problem with Crescent. If Crescent then refuses to recognize that this is the best strategy for the unit—and he must be given every opportunity to argue that growth is the correct option—replacing him becomes a possibility.

I hope Marlowe comes to realize that the real problem at Sargon is the inappropriate corporate strategy being pursued by Hestnes. (If he doesn't, he will soon find the organization under siege from Wall Street.) Crescent's objection to his role in the company is merely one manifestation of the problem. To replace Crescent would be to sacrifice to a misguided corporate strategy someone who might be a great manager.

➤ Jane Warner

Jane Warner is president of Randall Textron, a diversified manufacturing company based in Troy, Michigan. Before joining Textron, she held executive positions at General Motors in the manufacturing, engineering, and quality areas.

This scenario either represents the failure of Sargon's management to develop, communicate, and obtain support for a solid corporate strategy or is an example of a key division head's unwillingness or inability to change the focus of his business to achieve the company's overall objectives. Either way, Hestnes and Marlowe are not approaching the problem in a productive way. I suspect that Hestnes's judgment is clouded by his preference for high-tech products and by the fact that Arcell was established before his appointment as chairman of Sargon. I don't know what is causing Marlowe's confused thinking. But it's clear that if he doesn't bring Hestnes and Crescent together to share a common vision, he may be forced to move Crescent aside. And that would be a shame because Crescent is clearly a competent and respected leader.

Right now, Hestnes and Marlowe seem to be focusing on Crescent as the problem rather than considering how

Sargon functions vis-à-vis its business sectors' roles and goals. Their orientation leads me to believe that Sargon, as a corporate parent, has not developed robust top-level financial goals or a strong, supporting strategic plan. If that is the case, Crescent isn't the problem; he is merely a symptom. He is following the natural instinct of an executive to protect and grow his business, because he hasn't seen what Hestnes and Marlowe want Sargon to look like once the big investments in new businesses are completed. Hestnes and his management team—which should include Crescent, by the way—need to determine how Sargon plans to compete, how success will be measured, what roles various sectors will play, and how Sargon's transition will occur.

The very process of developing a comprehensive strategy for Sargon would clarify the company's expectations of Crescent and of Arcell. For example, the process of developing financial goals might confirm the need for Arcell to be a cash cow indefinitely. Or the management team might find that Arcell needs to be supported for a specified time while Sargon makes the transition to a predetermined business mix. In both cases, Arcell might need a certain amount of investment to sustain its performance. And in both cases, Crescent *would* be able to motivate his team and offer incentive compensation if he understood and accepted the rationale behind the plan.

In the extreme, Sargon's management team might decide that Arcell should be divested. That decision wouldn't necessarily result in a disaster. It has been my experience that if you are honest with people and show a sincere interest in their personal and professional needs, they will work with you through any circumstance. While open communication is always a key to success, a divestiture demands focused and frequent communication, with the parent company offering as much help as necessary with outplacement and severance.

On the other hand, the group might validate Crescent's interest in international expansion, Arcell might be recast as a potential global player, and that move in turn might open doors for growth in other sectors. There might be joint projects that could utilize the resources and expertise of two or more Sargon divisions and prove rewarding for everyone. Or there might be customers that Arcell could cultivate for other Sargon businesses. Textron's Avdel Division, a global supplier of engineered fasteners—designed for automotive and electronic uses, among others—has helped create a business relationship between Toyota and Textron's Randall Division. Avdel managers spotted potential connections, introduced the players, and, by virtue of their company's reputation, provided a good foundation on which to build the new partnerships.

Of course, it may prove difficult for the current management team to conceive a strategy on their own. Hestnes, Marlowe, and Crescent (along with other members of Sargon's top echelon, no doubt) have been together for a long time. It is hard to know whether questions being raised by Hestnes regarding Arcell and Crescent are a function of old patterns of interaction or whether the tensions exist because the company is in transition. It is clear that different skills and perspectives are required today than were needed in 1977, when Hestnes took the helm. For those reasons, and to depersonalize the issues further, Sargon would probably do well to consider hiring an outside resource to help with its competitive analysis, strategic planning, and executive staffing decisions.

However chartered, a written plan that includes such specifics as a five-year financial forecast, and goals and plans for specific sectors, is essential. Are there synergies among the businesses? What needs to be done with each sector to make it the top one or two in its field? All the senior managers—Crescent, the other Sargon division heads, and top-level staff officers—must be included in the process and be clear on their divisions' objectives in order for the plan to work.

If Sargon does have clear financial strategies and a supporting strategic plan that, at a minimum, was created with input from Crescent and the other division heads and has been well communicated throughout the organization, then Crescent may in fact be a problem. In that case, Marlowe needs to have a one-on-one with him—and soon. After Crescent's concerns are considered and, if appropriate, accommodated, his behavior needs to change. If he simply cannot be a team player in the context of the larger Sargon organization, Hestnes and Marlowe will need to move him out.

As for the car ride, Marlowe should discourage any specific mention of Crescent and instead focus the discussion on whether Sargon is following a well-defined and clearly communicated business plan. If Sargon has a strategy, is it the right one or does it need refinement? Have the company's goals been communicated? If the plan needs more development, Marlowe should take the lead in its planning and execution. If Hestnes and Marlowe believe that the best possible plan is in place and that it is well understood throughout the organization, the writing is on the wall for Crescent. But if they have any doubts about their strategy, they really are at the beginning of a long, rough road.

Originally published in September–October 1996

Reprint 96508

Go Global—or No?

Executive Summary

Greg McNally was up a creek. Literally. The CEO of software start-up DataClear was standing in the Alta River in Norway considering his options. Only a few weeks ago, he had called an off-site in Montana to celebrate his company's success in racking up $5 million in sales from its first product, ClearCloud—a powerful data analysis package. He had meant to use the meeting to consider expanding sales of ClearCloud from its current base in the telecommunications and financial services industries into the chemical, petrochemical, and pharmaceutical markets.

But that was before his talented and successful head of sales, Susan Moskowski, burst into his office with the news about VisiDat. It seemed that the British start-up was testing a data analysis package of its own that was only weeks away from launch. "We need to agree on a strategy for dealing with this kind of competition," Susan had told Greg. "If they start out as a global player, and we stay hunkered down in the U.S., they'll kill us."

Because of that news, Greg had changed the agenda of the off-site, instead having Susan present the options for taking DataClear global. The meeting had taken place two weeks ago, at which point the consensus had been to establish a European presence and probably one in Japan. The only question seemed to be whether to do it from scratch or to form partnerships with local players.

But as Greg stood in the Alta casting for salmon, a host of questions crowded in on him. Did DataClear really need to go global? Should it instead expand into different domestic markets? Should it do both at once? Could the company afford to? Four commentators offer their advice in this fictional case study.

"Why aren't they biting?" wondered Greg McNally as he laid down another perfectly executed cast. He was fly-fishing in the most beautiful spot he had ever seen, on the Alta in Norway—reputedly the home of Scandinavia's worthiest salmon. And he had plenty of opportunity to admire the view. No fish were getting in the way.

What a difference from the luck he'd had a couple of weeks earlier trout fishing at Nelson's Spring Creek in Montana. It seemed like so much more time had passed since the two-day off-site he had called there, designed to be part celebration of the past, part planning for the future.

Some celebration had definitely been in order. The company, DataClear, was really taking off, fueled by the success of its first software product, ClearCloud. In 1999, its first full year of operation, DataClear's sales reached $2.2 million. Now, the following September, it was looking like 2000 sales could easily reach $5.3 million. At the all-staff meeting on the Friday before the off-site, Greg had announced the company's success in recruiting two more great executives, bringing the staff to 38. "I'm more confident than ever that we'll hit our goals: $20 million in 2001 and then $60 million in 2002!"

Clouds on the Horizon

A New Jersey native, Greg held an MSc from Rutgers and then went West to get his PhD in computer science from UC Berkeley. He spent the next 15 years at Borland and Oracle, first as a software developer and then as a senior product manager. He started DataClear in Palo Alto, California, in the spring of 1998.

At that time, Greg realized that companies were collecting information faster than they could analyze it and that data analysis was an underexploited segment of the software business. It was at a seminar at Northwestern University that he saw his opportunity. Two researchers had developed a set of algorithms that enabled analysts to sift through large amounts of raw data in powerful ways without programmers' help. Greg cashed in his Oracle options and, in partnership with the two researchers, created DataClear to develop applications based on the algorithms.

His partners took responsibility for product development and an initial stake of 20% each; Greg provided $500,000 in financing in return for 60% of the shares and the job of CEO. A year later, Greg offered David Lester, founder of DL Ventures and a former

Oracle executive, 30% of the company in return for $5 million in additional funding.

In his previous positions, Greg had shown a knack for leading "fizzy" technical teams, and under his leadership, the two researchers came up with a state-of-the-art data analysis package they dubbed ClearCloud (from the clarity the software brought to large data clouds). Two versions, one for the telecommunications industry and the other for financial services providers, were officially launched in September 1998. ClearCloud had a number of immediate and profitable applications. For instance, it could be used to help credit card companies detect fraud patterns more quickly in the millions of transactions that occurred every day. Greg conservatively estimated the annual demand from the U.S. telecommunications and financial services sectors to be around $600 million. The challenge was to make potential users aware of the product.

ClearCloud was an instant hit, and within just a month of its launch, Greg had needed to recruit a dozen sales and service staffers. One of the first was Susan Moskowski, a former sales rep at Banking Data Systems, who had worked successfully with Greg on several major joint pitches to financial institutions. She had spent two years at BDS's Singapore subsidiary, where she had laid the groundwork for a number of important contracts. She had left BDS to do an MBA at Stanford and joined DataClear immediately on graduating as the new company's head of sales. She was an immediate success, landing DataClear's first major contract, with a large West Coast banking group.

Greg realized that ClearCloud had huge potential outside the telecommunications and financial services industries. In fact, with relatively little product development, Greg and his partners believed, ClearCloud could be adapted for the chemical, petrochemical, and pharmaceutical industries. Annual demand from customers in those sectors could reach as high as $900 million.

But accessing and serving clients in those fields would involve building specialized sales and service infrastructures. Just two months ago, to spearhead that initiative, Greg recruited a new business-development manager who had 20 years' experience in the chemical industry. A former senior R&D manager at DuPont, Tom Birmingham was excited by ClearCloud's blockbuster potential in the U.S. market. "The databases can only get bigger," he told Greg and Susan. Greg had asked Tom to put together a presentation for the offsite in Montana on the prospects for expanding into these new sectors.

Just two weeks before the outing, however, Susan burst into Greg's office and handed him an article from one of the leading trade journals. It highlighted a British start-up, VisiDat, which was beta testing a data analysis package that was only weeks away from launch. "We're not going to have the market to ourselves much longer," she told Greg. "We need to agree on a strategy for dealing with this kind of competition. If they start out as a global player, and we stay hunkered down in the U.S., they'll kill us. I've seen this before."

The news did not take Greg altogether by surprise. "I agree we've got to put together a strategy," he said. "Why don't we table the domestic-expansion discussion and talk about this at our off-site meeting, where we can get everyone's ideas? Unlike the rest of us, you've had some experience overseas, so perhaps you should lead the discussion. I'll square things with Tom."

Go Fish

In Montana, Susan kicked off the first session with the story of GulfSoft, a thinly disguised case study of her former employer. The company had developed a software package for the oil and gas exploration business, which it had introduced only in the United States. But at almost the same time, a French company had launched a comparable product, which it marketed aggressively on a global basis. A year later, the competitor had a much larger installed base worldwide than GulfSoft and was making inroads into GulfSoft's U.S. sales. When she reached the end of the story, Susan paused, adding ominously, "Today, we have only 20 installations of ClearCloud outside the U.S.—15 in the UK and five in Japan—and those are only U.S. customers purchasing for their overseas subsidiaries."

At Susan's signal, the room went dark. Much of what followed, in a blizzard of overhead projections, was market research showing a lot of latent demand for ClearCloud outside the United States. The foreign markets in telecommunications and financial services were shown to be about as large as those in the U.S.—that is, another $600 million. The potential in pharmaceuticals, petrochemicals, and chemicals looked to be about $660 million. Taken together, that meant a potential market of $1.5 billion domestically and $1.26 billion abroad.

In ending, Susan drew the obvious moral. "It seems pretty clear to me that the only defense for this kind of threat is to attack. We don't have any international sales strategy. We're here because we need one—and fast."

She glanced at Greg for any hint of objection, didn't see it, and plunged ahead: "We know we can sell a lot of software in the U.S., but if we want DataClear to succeed in the long run, we need to preempt the competition and go worldwide. We need a large installed base ASAP.

"I propose that for the afternoon we split into two groups and focus on our two options for going forward. Group A can consider building our own organization to serve Europe. Group B can think about forming alliances with players already established there. Based on what you come back with tomorrow, we'll make the call."

As the lights came back on, Greg blinked. He was dazzled. But he sensed that he needed to do some thinking, and he did his best thinking knee-deep in the river. After lunch, as the two groups got to work, Greg waded into Nelson's Spring Creek. The fish seemed to leap to his hook, but his thoughts were more elusive and ambivalent.

Money, Money, Money

Greg decided he needed a reality check, and that night he called David Lester to review the day's discussion. Not too surprisingly, Lester didn't have a lot of advice to give on the spot. In fact, he had questions of his own. "Instead of focusing on foreign markets in our core industries, what if we focus on developing ClearCloud for the domestic pharmaceutical, chemical, and petrochemical industries and capitalize on that $900 million U.S. market?" he asked. "How much would that cost?" Greg offered a best guess of $2 million for the additional software-development costs but hadn't yet come up with a number for marketing and sales; the industries were so different from the ones DataClear currently focused on. "Whatever the cost turns out to be, we're going to need another round of financing," Greg allowed. "Right now we're on track to generate a positive cash flow without raising any additional capital, but it won't be enough to fund a move beyond our core industries."

"That's not where I was headed," Lester replied. "What if we went out and raised *a lot* more money and expanded the product offering and our geographic reach at the same time?"

Greg swallowed hard; he was usually game for a challenge, but a double expansion was daunting. He couldn't help thinking of the sticky note he'd posted on the frame of his computer screen a few days after he started DataClear. It clung there still, and it had just one word on it: "Focus."

Lester sensed Greg's hesitation: "Look. We're not going to decide this tonight. And really, at the end of the day it's up to you, Greg. You've done the right things so far. Keep doing them." Hanging up, Greg was reminded of how pleased he was with Lester's hands-off approach. For the first time, he wondered what things would be like if he had a more hands-on venture capitalist as an investor—maybe one with some experience in international expansion.

Greg was also reminded of his own lack of international management experience. Eight years earlier, he had politely turned down an opportunity to lead a team of 50 Oracle development engineers in Japan, primarily because he had been unwilling to relocate to Tokyo for two years. His boss at the time had told him: "Greg, software is a global business, and what you don't learn early about cross-border management will come back to haunt you later."

Options on the Table

At ten o'clock the next morning, Group A took the floor and made their recommendation right off the bat: DataClear should immediately establish an office in the

UK and staff it with four to six salespeople. Britain would be a beachhead into all of Europe, but eventually there would also be a sales office somewhere on the Continent, maybe in Brussels. They had even drafted a job description for a head of European sales.

Greg was impressed, if a little overwhelmed. "Any idea how much this would cost us in terms of salaries and expenses over the first year?" he asked.

"Conservatively, about $500,000 a year; probably more," the group leader replied. "But cost is not so much the point here. If we don't make this move, we'll get killed by VisiDat—or some other competitor we don't even know about yet. Imagine if SAP introduced a similar product. With their marketing machine, they would just crush us."

Tom Birmingham started to object. "Where are we going to find local staff to install and support the product?" he wanted to know. "I mean, this is not just about setting up an office to sell: ClearCloud is a complex product, and it needs a service infrastructure. We'd have to translate the interface software, or at least the manuals, into local languages. We'd need additional resources in business development and product support to manage all this. Selling ClearCloud in Europe is going to cost a lot more than $500,000 a year—"

Susan was quick to jump in. "Good point, Tom, and that isn't all we'll need. We also have to have somebody in Asia. Either Singapore or Tokyo would be an ideal base. Probably Tokyo works better because more potential clients are headquartered there than in the rest of Asia. We need at least four people in Asia, for the time being." Tom frowned but, feeling that Susan had the momentum, decided to hold his fire.

After lunch, it was Group B's turn. They suggested using autonomous software distributors in each country. That would help DataClear keep a tight grip on expenses. Greg spoke up then. "What about teaming up with some local firm in Europe that offers a complementary product? Couldn't we get what we need through a joint venture?"

"Funny you should mention that, Greg," said the presenter from Group B. "We came up with the idea of Benro but didn't have time to pursue it. They might be willing to talk about reciprocal distribution." Benro was a small software shop in Norway. Greg knew it had made about $5 million in sales last year from its data-mining package for financial services companies. Benro was very familiar with European customers in the financial services sector but had no experience with other industries. "Working with Benro might be cheaper than doing this all on our own, at least for now," the presenter said.

Susan chose that moment to speak up again. "I have to admit I'm skeptical about joint ventures. I think it will probably take too long to negotiate and sign the contracts, which won't even cover all the eventualities. At some point we will have to learn how to succeed in each region on our own."

That's when Greg noticed Tom studying Susan, his eyes narrowing. So he wasn't surprised—in fact he was a little relieved—when Tom put the brakes on: "I guess I don't see how we can make that decision until we gather a little more input, Susan," Tom said. "At the very least, we need to have a conversation with Benro and any other potential partners. And I know I'd want to meet some candidates to lead a foreign sales office before I'd be comfortable going that route. But my real concern is more fundamental. Are we up to doing all this at the same time we're building our market presence in the U.S.? Remember, we don't yet have the capability to serve the chemical and pharmaceutical industries here. There are still only 38 of us, and I estimate that building the support infrastructure we need just for domestic expansion could cost as much $2 million—on top of product development."

Before Susan could object, Greg struck the compromise. "Tell you what. Let's commit to making this decision in no more than three weeks. I'll clear my calendar and connect with Benro myself. At the same time, Susan, you can flush out some good candidates for a foreign sales office and schedule them to meet with Tom and me."

Casting About

And that's how Greg McNally found himself up a creek in Norway that Sunday morning. Benro's CEO had been interested; Greg was confident that the meeting with him on Monday would yield some attractive options. And once the trip was booked, it didn't take

Greg long to realize that he'd be near some fabled fishing spots.

He also realized it would be a great chance to pick the brain of his old Berkeley classmate, Sarah Pappas. A hardware engineer, Sarah had started her own company, Desix, in Mountain View, California, in 1993. The company designed specialty chips for the mobile communications industry. Within seven years, Desix had grown into one of the most successful specialized design shops around the world, with about 400 employees. Like Greg, Sarah had received funding from a venture capitalist. Since a lot of demand for Desix's services was in Scandinavia and to a lesser degree in Japan as well, Sarah had opened subsidiaries in both places and even decided to split her time between Mountain View and Oslo.

Greg arrived in Oslo on Thursday morning and met Sarah that evening at a waterfront restaurant. They spent the first half-hour swapping news about mutual friends. Sarah hadn't changed much, thought Greg. But when the conversation turned to potential geographic expansion and he asked about her experience, Greg saw her smile grow a little tense. "Ah, well," she began. "How much time do you have?"

"That bad?"

"Actually, to be honest, some things were easier than we thought," she allowed. "Recruiting, for example. We never expected to get any great engineers to leave Nokia or Hitachi to join us, but we ended up hiring our Oslo and Tokyo core teams without much trouble. Still, some things turned out to be so hard— like coordinating the three sites across borders. There were so many misunderstandings between Oslo and Mountain View that at first our productivity went down by 40%."

The story got worse. Sarah explained how, in 1998, her venture capitalist sought to exit its investment. Since an IPO seemed inadvisable for various reasons, the parties agreed to sell the company to Pelmer, a large equipment manufacturer. Sarah agreed to stay on

"So you think you made the wrong choice in expanding internationally?"

for three years but couldn't do much to keep the engineers in her Oslo and Tokyo subsidiaries from leaving. No one had fully anticipated the clash between Pelmer's strong U.S. culture and Desix's local cultures in Oslo and Tokyo. By this point, Sarah felt, the merger had destroyed much that had gone into making Desix a small multinational company.

"I can tell I've been a real buzz killer," she laughed apologetically, as Greg picked up the check. "But if I were you, given what I've been through, I'd stay focused on the U.S. for as long as possible. You might not build the next Oracle or Siebel that way, but you'll live a happier life."

"So you think you made the wrong choice in expanding internationally?"

"Well, no," said Sarah, "because I don't think we had a choice. You, on the other hand, can sell much more product in the U.S. than we could have."

Up to His Waist

The next day brought its own worries, as Greg met with Pierre Lambert, a candidate for head of European sales, whom Susan had identified through a headhunter. Lambert had graduated from the Ecole des Mines in Paris and then worked for four years at Alcatel and five years at Lucent. As they talked, it occurred to Greg that he had no experience in reading résumés from outside the States. Was Ecole des Mines a good school? He noted that Lambert had worked only in France and the U.S. How successful would he be in the UK or Germany? As he wrapped up the interview, Greg figured he would need to see at least five candidates to form an opinion about the European labor market. And Asia would be even harder.

That evening, he compared notes with Tom, who had interviewed Lambert by phone the previous day. Tom expressed some doubts: he suspected that Lambert wasn't mature enough to deal with the level of executives—CIOs and chief scientists—that DataClear would be targeting. That call only just ended when the cell phone rang again, with Susan on the line. "Greg— I thought you would want to know. VisiDat just made its first significant sale—to Shell. The deal is worth at least $500,000. This is huge for them."

And now, two days later, here he stood in the glorious, frustrating Alta. He could see the salmon hanging just under the surface. He cast his line again, an elegant, silvery arc across the river and maneuvered the fly deftly through the water. Nothing.

Greg slogged back to shore and peered into the box housing his extensive collection of hand-tied salmon flies. Was it just that he was so preoccupied? Or were the conditions really so different here that none of his flies would work? One thing was for sure: it was a lot chillier than he'd expected. Despite the liner socks, his feet were getting cold.

Should DataClear Go Global?

Four commentators offer their advice.

➤ Heather Killen

Heather Killen is senior vice president of international operations at Yahoo!.

DataClear is facing a dilemma common to many small companies that realize they have a global opportunity on their hands. Should it take the plunge into new markets at the risk of overreaching its capabilities or stick to its knitting at the cost of missing key growth opportunities?

Greg doesn't have too much to work with. He and his team have little international operating or sales experience. His current VC has adopted a hands-off approach and is unlikely to be much help in plotting out an international strategy. What's more, the company may have to overcome technical difficulties. If DataClear has to reengineer the product so it can analyze data in other languages (especially two-byte languages like Japanese and Chinese) or use different data formats (commas instead of periods to indicate decimal places, for example), the road ahead will be long.

That said, remaining a domestic U.S. player is not an option. DataClear needs to take its business global. For a start, the company is not growing quickly enough, and it needs to move aggressively if it is to break out. What's more, if Greg is correct that the demand for data analysis services is about to explode, then the company could easily be scooped by established businesses entering the space or by better-funded start-ups.

A move abroad also fits with both DataClear's actual customers in the telecommunications and financial sectors and its potential customers in the petrochemical and pharmaceutical industries. Many of the players in these industries are based outside the United States (DataClear's first real competitor, VisiDat, has just sold its product to Shell, a global enterprise that's not based in the States).

It makes no sense to distinguish between the "U.S." and the "international" markets. Rather than ask whether they should expand overseas, Greg and his team should ask whether customers will want to implement DataClear's product on a global basis. The case gives us little to go on, but if we assume that they will, then, once again, that's a strong argument for moving abroad. After all, DataClear needs to reach its customers wherever decisions about global investments are being made.

However, the expansion alternatives presented in the case are not attractive, and Greg needs to review his options more thoroughly. Building international sales offices from scratch could be expensive and may not yield much in the way of concrete results. On the face of it, an alliance strategy is more promising—but choosing a joint-venture partner is a difficult process. What's more, Greg has already given up a fairly large slice of his equity in the company to DL Ventures, so he needs to be judicious about the partners he brings into the business at this stage. Benro is clearly a nonstarter. As a small niche player, it doesn't have the juice to help DataClear.

There are, however, other options. Targeting global companies based in the United States could be a good way to begin to expand overseas. In fact, DataClear has already made a start in this direction; several U.S. customers have purchased the product for their foreign subsidiaries. (This also suggests that the product may be fairly easily adapted to conditions outside the States.) Greg should also seek out a powerful channel partner with connections to non-U.S. markets. SAP, mentioned as a possible competitor, could also be a good partner in view of its strong European orientation. In fact, co-opting SAP as a partner before it becomes a competitor would be a smart move. Finally, Greg should consider looking for fresh input and capital from a strong VC in Europe or Asia. That would help DataClear get incubation support for a more daring go-it-alone approach.

➤ Alison Sander

Alison Sander is a manager in the Boston office of the Boston Consulting Group and serves as BCG's global topic leader.

DataClear has a product with international potential, but Greg is on the verge of making three classic mistakes in evaluating his options. The first is going global for reactive instead of strategic reasons. The second is basing a decision on numbers that seriously underestimate the costs of international expansion. The third is gravitating toward obvious and expensive approaches rather than examining a full range of options.

Greg needs to clarify his rationale for global expansion and consider a broader range of tactical options. VisiDat's sale to Shell is not reason enough to refocus DataClear's strategy on overseas alternatives. An international strategy should be based on at least one of three competitive advantages:

- arbitrage—leveraging advantages available in specific countries (for instance, low-cost capital or labor, special expertise, or favorable tax positions);

- strategic positioning—preempting a competitor, gaining a first-mover advantage, or locking in favorable terms with suppliers;

- replicability—reproducing a product or a business model cost-effectively in many countries in order to gain scale advantages.

DataClear appears to have no arbitrage advantage. The company really has no strategic-positioning advantage either, even though the main rationale presented is that DataClear should preempt VisiDat in order to defend its strategic position. VisiDat is oriented toward the oil and gas market rather than DataClear's financial services market. Defending a strategic position is expensive, and until Data-Clear builds a bigger war chest, such a move may divert management's attention from the immediate priority of selecting markets where DataClear can build profitable market share quickly. Indeed, Susan's focus on VisiDat appears to have obscured her best argument for going global: the opportunity to profitably replicate DataClear's existing software product. But a far more thorough analysis is required before a replication strategy can be developed, as the competitive challenges of and opportunities for building profitable operations vary widely from country to country.

Building a successful global strategy would also require Greg to take a much closer look at the cost estimates. For a start, he hasn't factored in the typical costs for software adaptation, such as local product customization and support. What's more, the company has focused on two of the world's most expensive markets in which to set up operations: London and Tokyo. Finally, as Sarah points out, global complexity comes with unexpected administrative and coordination costs.

If Greg does decide to go global, he needs to look beyond the options presented in the case. Establishing an overseas subsidiary is expensive. And while a joint venture would cost less and bring in new knowledge and capabilities, the poor track record of most joint ventures suggests that Data-Clear needs to evaluate its potential partners more systematically. An ill-conceived alliance with Benro could prove as risky as competing against VisiDat; Benro also serves the financial services sector and could develop capabilities through the venture that would let it compete with Data-Clear.

Fortunately, Greg does not have to choose between those two options. Lower-cost alternatives do exist: licensing ClearCloud, selling it on the Web, or hiring a local sales representative, for instance. Perhaps the smartest option, however, would be to continue with the strategy that is already working: selling to financial institutions that are purchasing for their overseas subsidiaries. By targeting global companies like Visa or MasterCard, DataClear could leverage those customers' existing global infrastructures. Instead of investing in overseas offices, Greg could hire a manager in the United States to supervise sales and develop customized support for large multinational customers. The best-run companies follow a step-by-step approach to global expansion.

➤ Barry Schiffman

Barry Schiffman is president and executive managing director at JAFCO America Ventures, a venture capital firm based in Palo Alto, California, and Boston.

G reg is facing a common strategic threat: the possibility that a competitor will beat his company to overseas markets with a similar or better product. A more-established company would be wise to preempt the threat as soon as it can. But as a fledgling start-up, DataClear does not yet have the personnel or capital to support an international venture. Unless Greg and his team take a lot more time than they seem to wish to do, they may well find that they'll spend a lot of money without getting a single international order.

For a start, DataClear does not have a manager who can spearhead a move abroad. To pursue that option, the company would need a senior executive with five to six years' experience in the target markets and a mastery of at least one relevant foreign language. At present, the only executive with any international experience is Susan—and hers was just two years in Asia, not Europe. Greg may be tempted to strike a compromise by putting Susan in charge of the expansion on an interim basis while searching for someone with the right experience. But going that route would be unwise. DataClear would be likely to lose domestic business without winning enough foreign business to compensate.

Second, DataClear needs more capital. Global expansion tends to be a long, drawn-out war. International sales teams (especially in non-English-speaking markets) take a long time to close their first deal. Even when they have a well-developed product, they still have to customize it to suit local needs and establish distribution channels. When the California-based software company BroadVision, for instance, set up its Japanese subsidiary in 1997, it had to wait about two years before it was able to realize any value from the venture. In the meantime, it had to support the subsidiary from its U.S. operations.

DataClear doesn't have the capacity to support a move abroad from current operations; it will have to raise cash from its investors to cover the costs—as Lester and Greg recognize. That means coming up with a convincing business plan, which Greg is far from being able to do at present.

For these reasons, I do not recommend that Greg go along with Susan's evident determination to head up an immediate international expansion initiative. But he would certainly be well advised to invest some money in a feasibility study in the next three to six months. I would suggest that he hire a consulting firm to do a detailed analysis of the opportunities in both Europe and Asia. Working with the consultants, Greg should spend a few days himself in each of his initial target markets and meet face-to-face with potential partners and customers.

At the same time, DataClear needs to understand its potential competitors a lot better than it currently seems to. There are plenty of unanswered questions. Is VisiDat the only threat? How real is the $500,000 order from Shell? Is that a big order in the petrochemical market? How long will it take to convert ClearCloud to compete with VisiDat's product in that market? Thus far, DataClear's competitive analysis seems to be limited to reading news articles and press releases from the competition.

If the results of these market research efforts are encouraging, DataClear should immediately approach its investors with a two- to three-year business plan. When its funding is in place, the company should recruit a new executive to head its international operations. In the meantime, DataClear might benefit from continuing to build close relationships in its domestic markets with customers that have a strong international presence or at least global brand recognition. Names like Sprint, Citigroup, and

Microsoft spring to mind. Having references from companies like these will make it much easier for DataClear to get its foot in the door with overseas customers.

➤ Scott Schnell

Scott Schnell is senior vice president of marketing and corporate development at RSA Security, a software company based in Bedford, Massachusetts.

DataClear is facing a decision that sooner or later every new business must face. But any expansion plan must be fully understood in the context of a company's existing strengths, its management experience and talent, and its current and future opportunities. Greg is in danger of allowing himself to be rushed into a decision without taking the time for responsible due diligence—and his celebratory off-site has been transformed into a crusade to solve an issue that does not need an immediate resolution.

In fact, a move abroad at this time makes questionable strategic sense. In DataClear's market, it is much more important to focus on cementing a position of strength in the United States—where the company has an early lead in the largest, most-promising territory—than to be the first to market in all possible territories. Businesses win by building from a strong, defensible market position with a top-performing product and a supporting organizational infrastructure. To spend so much of senior management's time on aggressively establishing foreign operations when the company has not yet fortified its home base is a recipe for failure. A $5 million, 38-person company like DataClear does not seem to have a strong enough base of strength, given the potential size of the markets involved.

From an organizational perspective, DataClear's lack of planning demonstrates that management is not ready for the challenges involved in building an international business. The company has not even developed a strategy or a time line for expansion into new domestic markets. And no company should guide its actions solely on the press releases, rumors, and sales triumphs of competitors, especially when selling a sophisticated product with a long sales cycle like ClearCloud.

Worse, DataClear is worryingly thin on international experience. Greg admits he doesn't know what it would take to be a good head of European sales. The only person with any international seasoning is Susan, but her judgment seems to be clouded by BDS's bad experience in Singapore. She has failed to realize how different BDS's situation was from the one that DataClear now faces. BDS was already an international company and could easily have sold its new product overseas had it decided to—it just unwisely chose not to. For DataClear, however, going abroad represents a much greater challenge.

At some point, of course, DataClear will have to expand internationally, and in my experience, its best alternative will be forming joint ventures or partnerships with value-added resellers—not establishing its own international presence as a first step. In this respect, Greg's instinct is quite sound. But before talking to companies like Benro, Greg and his team need to think carefully about the markets and partners they should choose. How do DataClear's current target segments differ in the United States, Europe, and Asia? Should the company look for partners that have similar product experience in adjacent markets or ones that serve DataClear's traditional customers with other products? How many partners should DataClear have in Europe? What sort of partnership structure will best align the incentives of the partners involved?

Finally, Greg should not delegate the task of devising an international plan to Tom and Susan. Given their strongly different views on expansion, their joint efforts could disintegrate into a power struggle. Instead, Greg should lead the planning effort himself and allow two to three months to formulate a strategy. For help in learning about foreign markets, Greg should look outside the company to colleagues, investors, and specialists—as indeed he has started to do with Lester and Sarah. The challenge Greg faces is daunting, but it is not immediate, and a panic reaction will only make matters worse.

Originally published in June 2001

Reprint R0106A

THOMAS J. WAITE

Stick to the Core—

or Go for More?

George Caldwell, cofounder of Advaark, a cutting-edge ad agency, was listening hard to his biggest client, John McWilliams, CEO of GlobalBev. McWilliams ran a multibillion-dollar holding company for an assortment of food and beverage brands but was giving credit to Advaark for his latest product line. "We were completely blindsided by this whole 'energy drink' craze," McWilliams was saying, clearly delighted that Advaark had steered his company into the business. Then he enthused, "I'd love to get your thinking about our snack lines."

"Oh, no," George thought. He hadn't realized that his partner, Ian Rafferty, had made this foray into

Executive Summary

strategic consulting. Traditionally, their agency focused only on the creative execution of ad campaigns. In fact, they'd disagreed before about whether it was wise to follow customers' needs into areas where they had no skills advantage. George thought Advaark should stick to its core competence. Ian saw a source of easy revenue and an enhanced offering to clients who, he claimed, wanted one-stop shopping.

The potential was appealing, but for George, it hardly outweighed the downsides. They'd risk alienating the strategy companies that now referred clients to Advaark. They'd need to recruit or develop new kinds of talent and create a methodology and training. George was just deciding to nix the expansion when a chance meeting with a former client made him pause. She'd heard about GlobalBev's success and wanted the same kind of help. Eager to win back a lapsed account, George was tempted.

Should Advaark meet more of its customers' needs by expanding its services or stay focused on what it does best? Four commentators weigh in on this fictional case.

"Cut!" Spike Sanchez stomped toward the stage, his arms waving the music to a stop. Wearing black from head to toe, sporting dark glasses, and sweating under the heat of the lights, he was losing his patience. A highly respected music video director, Sanchez was starting to wonder if taking on this advertising gig was such a great idea. "How many times do I have to tell you to point the logo on the can *toward* the camera during that move?"

On stage was Maygan M, a pop singer whose star had risen in the months since she'd agreed to do this ad. She was a sweet-faced, 18-year-old beauty, dressed in a sequined, midriff-baring halter top, a skintight leopard microskirt, and platform shoes that had already tripped her up twice. She sheltered her eyes from the lights and glared at Sanchez. "Like I can even see the stupid logo," she whined. "Maybe you could fix it on a computer or something?"

"Or maybe you should just do what I say," Sanchez shot back. "Then we might have some hope of airing this 30-second spot before your 15 minutes of fame are up!" He turned abruptly, strode off the stage, and dropped back into his director's chair. "Let's try it again from the top." Maygan pouted at him for a moment and then flipped her long hair, spun around, and went back to her starting position.

Sitting next to Sanchez was Ian Rafferty, cofounder and head of creative services for Advaark, a New York-based advertising agency. "Pretty tough to work with, isn't she?" he whispered.

"This?" Sanchez waved his hand dismissively. "This is nothing! Try working with some rock 'n' roll dinosaur strung out on crank and wanting to make a comeback!"

In the back of the studio, Rafferty's partner and fellow founder George Caldwell was deep in conversation with John McWilliams, the CEO of GlobalBev. Both men were oblivious to the antics onstage. One of Advaark's key clients, GlobalBev was a multibillion-dollar holding company for an assortment of well-known food and beverage brands.

"We were completely blindsided by this 'energy drink' craze," McWilliams was saying to Caldwell. A relatively new beverage category, energy drinks touted their herbal stimulants and got an extra jolt from loads of caffeine and sugar. Teens and 20-somethings all pounded them back while studying, exercising, and dancing and used them to get a kick start in the morning. They couldn't seem to get enough of the stuff. "But thanks to this," McWilliams continued with a nod toward the stage, "I think we're going to get into the game in a hurry. What a name, huh? *Nirvoza!* Is that great or what?"

Caldwell was about to say something when the music began to blare again and Maygan resumed her lip-synching routine. As he watched her and the dancers prance around the stage, he thought about the conversation he'd had with Rafferty over the brand name. He didn't like it. It made him think of anorexia—not a good vibe, even for Advaark's cutting-edge style of advertising.

But Rafferty had persuaded him with the results of a market test. The Nirvoza brand had scored incredibly high with the drink's target audience, who liked the fact that it suggested nirvana and nervousness at the same time. Some mentioned that it had echoes of the Seattle grunge band, Nirvana. Even though the group's singer had committed suicide, Rafferty wasn't concerned. The people who made that association, he argued, were the very people who would like an even edgier feel to the brand. Caldwell was finally swayed. And clearly the client was pleased with the choice.

Suddenly the music stopped and Maygan M thrust the can toward the camera right on cue. "Achieve your *own* Nirvoza!" she snarled. Everyone was silent until Sanchez bolted upright and stretched his arms out wide. "Unbelievable," he shouted. "She did it!" Then he smiled. "Okay, everyone. That's a wrap." There was scattered applause as Sanchez turned and clapped Rafferty on the back. "I'll check out the tape before we send it over," he said. "But I think we nailed it."

"Great. Thanks, Spike." Rafferty got up and headed toward McWilliams and Caldwell, who were still huddled together at the back of the studio.

"You know, George," McWilliams was saying, "I've always been impressed with Advaark's creative work. The stuff you've done for us over the years has been absolutely great. But you should've told me earlier that you also help your clients decide whether to get into new markets." Caldwell was just about to ask McWilliams what he was talking about when Rafferty joined them.

"So," Rafferty said, looking at both of them, "Whad'ja think?"

"It's great!" said McWilliams enthusiastically. "And I can only thank you again for recommending that we get into energy drinks. I have a really good feeling about this. By the way, when we've completely wrapped up this campaign, I'd love to get your thinking about our snack lines. I can't put my finger on it, but I think we're missing something there. Okay?"

Rafferty shot a quick glance at Caldwell and then nodded at McWilliams. "Sure. And in the meantime, here's something you might want to stick in your trophy case." He handed him the Nirvoza can, personally crushed by Maygan M.

Core Combatants

As McWilliams walked out the studio door, Caldwell turned to Rafferty. "Was it really you who steered

GlobalBev toward the energy drink market? I thought it was his idea."

Rafferty frowned. "Actually, that's something I've been meaning to talk to you about. It was clear to me that that market was on the verge of exploding and that GlobalBev was going to miss out on it. It's not like we don't understand their business, George. So I suggested to McWilliams that we take a closer look at it."

"And?"

"He said to go ahead. So we did a bunch of research on the energy drink market and its projected growth rate and figured out the existing competition. It all added up to a good move for GlobalBev. I showed our findings to John and he loved it. End of story."

Caldwell respected Rafferty's track record of successes, but he wasn't pleased with this kind of maverick behavior. "First of all, Ian, we're partners. I should have been apprised of all this. And second, did it ever occur to you that the energy drink market might be just a passing fad?"

"Don't worry, George. We did our homework. Even if the market tanks in three years, which I don't think it will, GlobalBev will still make a killing with Nirvoza. They've already got all the manufacturing capabilities and distribution channels in place. This could be huge for them."

Caldwell was upset, but Rafferty was a brilliant creative talent, and clients loved him. He chose his words carefully. "Ian, I do applaud your initiative. But when we formed this business, we agreed that the key to our long-term success was staying focused on what we do best—creating unforgettable ads. It's really important that we not wander from what makes us great."

Rafferty scarcely needed the reminder that Advaark's strength was creative. He and Caldwell had formed the agency seven years ago when, bored with mindless jingles and sweepstakes promotions, they left the multinational ad giant that had employed them both for a decade. Their own reputations and their accumulated Clios led them right away to some high-profile accounts. They hired gifted writers and artists (and more than a few oddballs) and gave free rein to their inspired lunacy and offbeat ideas. Rafferty was the ringmaster, a flamboyant visionary who was never content with the status quo. But equally important were Caldwell's sharp focus and operational skills. Together, the partners created an effective balance. And Advaark quickly developed a reputation for "water cooler" ads—the kind that got people talking.

As word got out that Advaark was uniquely successful in getting the attention of sophisticated—even jaded—consumers, the firm's revenues soared. Despite Advaark's rapid growth to a midsize firm with annual billings of $550 million and almost 400 people, the company managed to maintain a culture in which innovation thrived. Advaark was a magnet for all kinds of creative people.

And now, Ian was proposing a change that could threaten all that. "But I know we can be great at this," he insisted. "We didn't charge for it this time, but can you imagine what something like this would be worth to clients? If we packaged it up as a new service and sold it, we could generate a whole new stream of revenue."

"That's not the business we're in."

"Would you still say that if one of our competitors began offering it?"

Caldwell, late for a meeting already, nearly gave a dismissive wave of his hand as he started to turn away. Then it struck him how serious his partner was. "Look. We're still on for lunch, right? Let's talk about it then."

Airing Concerns

Dodging an in-line skater, Caldwell bounded up the steps of O-Zone, an oxygen bar with vegetarian specials that was Rafferty's favorite lunch spot. Rafferty was already seated, studying the list of the day's specials. Spotting Caldwell, he waved him over. "You're in luck—the lavender air is only a buck a minute!"

Caldwell laughed. "Hey, does this place serve hot dogs?"

By the time their orders arrived, though, the conversation had turned sober. "Ian, we're not even close to being experts in opening up new markets. Are you seriously proposing that we develop and launch a completely different service offering?"

"Why not?" countered Rafferty. "Take your blinders off, George. A lot is happening in our industry. It's consolidating—fast. More and more agencies are offering their clients one-stop shopping for a bunch of services, not just advertising." He paused to dip a carrot stick in hummus. "It's not even clear what an advertising firm really is any more. The lines are blurring between what we do and what other professional services firms do."

"But Ian, that's why focus is more important now than ever. We're an advertising firm, not a strategy consulting firm, remember? We've succeeded by being the best creative agency out there."

"We know we want to grow, and here we have a client begging us to provide it with a new service. Why on earth wouldn't we do that?"

"I'm sorry, George. I think we're in danger of resting on our laurels. If we only focus on what we've done in the past, we could blow our future. We need to change with the times."

Caldwell didn't agree. He reminded Rafferty of the last time they'd considered branching out into a new business—interactive advertising. That was the same kind of proposition, to Caldwell's mind: a chance to chase clients' needs into an arena where the firm had no skills advantage. After a heated debate, he had nixed the idea. And history, he believed, had proved him right. The Internet bubble had burst, and companies had abandoned their interactive agencies in droves. Advaark might have forgone some easy revenue, but it held on to its reputation—and its clients.

Rafferty let out a sigh. "Okay, okay, enough about the past. Let's talk about the future. We know we want to grow, and here we have a client begging us to provide it with a new service. Why on earth wouldn't we do that?" Advaark knew its clients' brands deeply, he pointed out, and had earned their trust. There was no reason to believe the service he was describing couldn't be sold to just about any of them. The revenue potential was obvious and particularly attractive because doing more business with existing clients would reduce the overall cost of sales. At the same time, the new offering might even attract whole new clients.

"And what if we screw up?" asked Caldwell. "What do you think will happen to our long-term client relationships then?" He proceeded to rattle off any number of reasons the venture might well fail: the lack of a standard methodology or training program, the risk of alienating the strategy consultants that regularly referred clients, the greater penalties associated with failure on any given project. And one challenge was particularly troubling to him. Advaark would need to recruit different kinds of talent, probably folks who didn't come cheap, and attracting and keeping them would likely require a different compensation scheme.

"So? We can do that," Ian argued. "All we'd need to do is price the service accordingly to cover that and maintain our margins. Hell, we may even see improvements in them."

"Slow down a minute, Ian. How's that going to go over with the rest of our people? Suddenly, they're second-class citizens? There's no question it would create a real cultural rift."

"You're not giving our people enough credit for being grown-ups. I'm telling you, if we don't create this kind of service, we risk becoming a second-class *firm*. You know the key to our future success is to grow our business by getting more share of the customer."

"No, Ian," Caldwell snapped back. "The key to our future success is to continue to do world-class work!"

A few nearby diners glanced over, possibly resenting the negativity being introduced into the air around them. Rafferty stared at Caldwell, then averted his eyes. He looked out the window and sighed. "All right, George. How about this? Let me do what I'd do for a client. I'll research this a little further. It sounds like you need more data."

Caldwell looked at Rafferty. It was a reasonable request. "Okay, Ian," he said, reaching for the check and pulling out his wallet. "Take a shot at it. And I promise I'll keep an open mind about it." Although he doubted Rafferty would be able to convince him, he wanted to make sure that his partner felt he was given an adequate hearing.

Data and Doubts

A week later, Rafferty presented his findings to Caldwell. They indicated that the market for marketing strategy services in the United States alone was conservatively estimated at $1.3 billion and projected to grow at an annual rate of at least 16% over the next five years. In addition, the companies currently serving this market were highly diverse, ranging from business strategy consulting firms to market research houses—and a couple of advertising agencies had even entered the arena. This, Rafferty argued, was not only a huge opportunity for Advaark but was also a warning to get moving before more agencies stepped up to the plate.

In deference to Caldwell's concerns about risk, he recommended that Advaark move slowly into the market by developing a service squarely aimed at the consumer products industry. Over half of the firm's clients were in that sector, and Advaark could take what it had learned from the GlobalBev experience and build on it. He concluded by presenting a time line for developing the service and outlining the capital investment that would be needed.

Caldwell had to admit he was impressed. Rafferty had put together a solid business case, and he appreciated the recommendation that they begin by focusing on only one industry segment. Still, the idea of launching a service they knew nothing about simply because one client had asked for it seemed risky. He asked Ian if he could have some time to think about it. Rafferty brightened a bit and handed over a copy of his study for Caldwell to read in detail.

As he headed to his fitness club that evening, Caldwell concluded that Rafferty had built the strongest possible case, but it still wasn't enough to convince him. Advaark was successful because of its laserlike focus on being the best creative agency. Wandering into the business strategy arena could be a disaster.

He pumped quickly on a cross-training machine, momentarily distracted by the pounding music and TV screens. When his time was up, he toweled off and headed for the juice bar, nearly bumping into Nancy Gilbert, an ex-client.

"George! I've been meaning to call you," she exclaimed, smiling broadly. Gilbert was the CEO of Botanic Beauties, a natural skin and hair products company. For five years, Botanic Beauties had been a flagship client of Advaark, but last year, Gilbert had put the account up for review. Advaark had worked tirelessly to keep the business but ended up losing to an upstart boutique based in Boston. It was an embarrassing loss for Advaark and blemished its otherwise solid reputation for long-term client relationships.

"Nancy. Good to see you," Caldwell masked his surprise. "What's up?"

"I was at a CEO roundtable yesterday and just happened to be sitting next to John McWilliams of Global-

Bev. He told me your firm was responsible for their decision to get into the energy drink market. And he was raving about the upcoming launch of Nirvoza."

Caldwell cleared his throat. "Well, that was very kind of him," he said evenly.

"Anyway, George, let me cut to the chase. We're thinking of going into toothpaste, and we need some guidance. I'd love to hear about your work in this area and how you might be able to help us."

Caldwell's head was spinning. Not only did a current client want Advaark to offer a strategic service, but now a former client did, too. Did Rafferty have the right idea after all?

Should Advaark Stick to Its Core Competence?

Four commentators offer expert advice.

➤ Gordon McCallum

Gordon McCallum is the group strategy director at Virgin Management, located in London.

How many service businesses have wrestled with this dilemma! Do you stick to your knitting or explore new sources of revenue? In this case, George Caldwell needs to understand that he's not just facing a strategic dilemma. He's also facing an organizational one. As risky as the new venture might be, it's less so than the prospect of alienating Ian Rafferty—which would likely lead, sooner or later, to the breakup of Advaark's great founding team.

It's easy to see why Caldwell is tempted to stay with the tried-and-true. He and his partner have built an exceptionally successful agency. Advaark's core competence is creativity, delivered by a focused and experienced team. Caldwell's instincts tell him that the company would be mad to branch out into ancillary services—and he's already had this view confirmed during Rafferty's previous interest in interactive advertising. He knows that the more the firm gets distracted by new initiatives, the more likely it will lose its touch. Much better to stay focused, even if it means slower growth.

But, of course, it's not that simple. It could be, after all, that Rafferty is right. Nirvoza is poised for a big splash. And the chance encounter with Nancy Gilbert implies that Advaark's other clients might eagerly embrace help in this area, which traditional consultancies may not be effectively serving. Perhaps it's also true that the whole sector will continue to consolidate around a smaller number of more broadly integrated service businesses. Most important, Rafferty's talents and charisma mesh well with making such a new business succeed.

For us at Virgin, this last point would weigh heavily in the decision. Like most venture capital companies, we have always put the ability and energy of the management teams that run our various businesses at the top of our checklist. While there are always other factors that determine success (business model, brand strength, industry structure, and competitive intensity, to name some of the more important), time and again we have found that the abilities of the people leading the organization determine whether we end up with a pig or a pony.

If I were Caldwell, I would let Rafferty test his idea but in a way that minimizes the downside risk. The leap from creative advertising to new product and marketing services is not huge, particularly if Rafferty focuses on those aspects that relate closely to brand development and management. He should steer clear of areas in which he lacks credentials and where multiple companies exist with specialized skills, such as quantitative research. Rafferty has put together a workable plan that needs only limited resources—and will have a limited impact if it fails.

Caldwell should give Rafferty very specific deliverables and, if possible, insulate him from "business as usual" by providing him with dedicated office space and a strong team to support him. If Rafferty succeeds, Advaark also wins and Caldwell's relationship with his partner is bolstered (at least until Rafferty's next big idea). If the trial fails, Rafferty knows he's given it his best shot, and his relationship with Caldwell may still be strengthened by the experience—especially if Caldwell manages the situation with care. With some skillful PR, the agency wouldn't suffer unduly.

Advaark operates in an industry in which creativity—one of the key requirements for success—is the scarcest resource. The partners know they must maintain an environment that's appealing to very talented individuals. As part of this, Caldwell has to loosen the reins and give Rafferty his head or risk losing a very creative partner—too high a price to pay for focus.

➤ John O. Whitney

John O. Whitney is a professor of management at Columbia Business School in New York. He joined the faculty there in 1986. He is the author of "Strategic Renewal for Business Units" (Harvard Business Review, July–August, 1996).

The late David Ogilvy, one of the world's great ad men, told about the time he was working for Aron Streit, the matzo company, and his client began editing the advertising copy. Ogilvy would have none of it. "Mr. Streit," he advised, "You make the matzos. I'll make the ads." The same wisdom applies here: Advaark should focus on ad making and stay out of the matzo business. Sure, the firm can offer ideas as part of its service to clients. But it's one thing to think up an idea and quite another to successfully bring that idea to market.

If Advaark is going to get into the business of advocating new food products, its staff should at least educate itself enough to ask good questions about food chemistry, FDA regulations, labeling laws in the states the products will appear, and manufacturing processes. And how about packaging? Should the new drink be in glass or plastic? Long neck or wide mouth? Screw cap, cork, or traditional bottle cap? Good product managers know, intimately, the capabilities and constraints of the product's manufacturers. How about test markets? Someone unfamiliar with these parameters could send product development on a wild goose chase. And how about distribution? Should it focus on convenience stores, supermarkets, vending machines, or mass merchants? These are just a few of the hundreds of decisions that will need to get made. A mistake in any one of them could spell doom for a new product and wasted resources for Advaark and its client.

Sound strategy can only result when managers have realistic expectations, derived from the external world, that help them know what to do and how to do it. They succeed when they are able to match those plans with the right resources and the will to carry a plan through to completion. Rafferty might have the will, but he appears to have little else. There's no evidence that he knows what to do and how to do it or that he even has the resources to pull it off.

Is this to say that Advaark, or any company for that matter, should never try out new ventures? Of course not. But if it does, it should form a new business—replete with infrastructure and resources—rather than append it to the existing enterprise. Appendages dilute the focus, energy, and accountability of management and in the process short-change both the core business and the new venture. Of course, as an alternative to taking the time and effort to develop its own product strategy business, Advaark could acquire an existing company. It *could*, but—assuming the case is set in the present day—I would say it should not.

Because Advaark may not know it, but its core business is at risk and requires the immediate and undivided attention of management.

Sadly, Advaark can take nothing for granted about its competitive advantage because the world has abruptly changed since September 11. No longer are people talking at the water cooler about clever advertising, and strategies that worked before may no longer work. Maygan M and all she stands for may suddenly seem meaningless and

---

The corporate junk pile is littered with companies that overlooked risks to their core business while pursuing new opportunities.

---

even distasteful. So Advaark's priority should be to identify changes in the mood and motivation of its clients' customers—and to explore ways of adapting to those changes.

It's an example of the moment, but a timeless concern nonetheless. The corporate junk pile is littered with companies that overlooked risks to their core business while pursuing new opportunities. The scarcest resources in any company are knowledgeable, experienced people who possess leadership skills. Any time a company engages in a strategic shift, those resources tend to be diverted from the core business.

Of course, there is a time for companies to diversify, to seek new markets, to engage in new activities. Economic and intellectual growth is essential to every enterprise. But the resources needed to achieve this growth must be identified, understood, and known to be available. Advaark's proposed new enterprise does not meet these requirements.

➢ Roland T. Rust

Roland T. Rust holds the David Bruce Smith Chair in Marketing at the University of Maryland's Robert H. Smith School of Business in College Park, Maryland. He is also the director of the Center for E-Service at the business school. He is the author of Driving Customer Equity: How Customer Lifetime Value Is Reshaping Corporate Strategy *(Free Press, 2000) with Valarie A. Zeithaml and Katherine N. Lemon.*

Like many companies today, Advaark finds itself trying to figure out whether to become more of a service organization. Caldwell views the company through its core competence, reflecting an inside-outward, internally focused orientation. Advaark does ad production well, so he concludes that that's what it should continue to focus on. Rafferty, on the other hand, sees the agency in terms of its customers, essentially an externally focused orientation. For him, the question is, what good is core competence if it's not what customers want?

The wave of the future is with Rafferty. Smart companies everywhere—first, in the services sector and now in the goods sector—are thinking less about product transactions and more about customer relationships. The goal is to increase an organization's "customer equity," the sum of a customer's lifetime value, across all of a company's customers.

My colleagues and I have conducted research that suggests three main drivers of customer equity. For Advaark, the first driver, value equity, will be built as the agency provides more value to its customers through the new service. The second, brand equity, will be achieved when Advaark broadens its image. Its brand will come to stand for an ability not only to create hip advertising but also to identify trendy new markets. The third, relationship equity, can be built by intensifying connections with clients and building knowledge about each one, thereby increasing their switching costs. Some marketers would refer to this as retention equity or "lock-in."

Expanding beyond core competence is not easy. I recently consulted for two multinational companies—a European food, chemicals, and consumer goods conglomerate and a U.S. chemical and biotech company—facing challenges similar to Advaark's. Each was grappling with how to transform old-line, transaction-oriented businesses into full-service, relationship-oriented business units. In each case, despite top management's best intentions, considerable internal resistance had developed because some key executives had become process-oriented and locked into the existing core competence.

Internally oriented companies think first about operational efficiency, so in difficult economic times, the tendency is to cut back on expansion and to reduce risk. The parts of the business that rely on customer relationships, which take time to nurture and build, may appear to be expendable, especially in their early stages when the relationships are not yet well established. Thus, the internally oriented business, used to reducing productive capacity in bad times to make immediate profit gains, may try to make equally drastic cutbacks in the relationship parts of its business, thereby nipping relationships in the bud. Building customer equity requires patience and continuity, especially in bad economic times.

If Advaark decides to go with the new service, a fundamental shift in how it sees its business must occur. It should now be a provider of services, first, and an ad factory, second. It will need to actively seek even more ways to invest in and deepen relationships with customers.

Caldwell already recognizes the complementarity of his and his partner's skills—Rafferty has the external, creative vision while Caldwell's own strengths are in operations. Rafferty should be given free rein to bring Advaark's business into line with what customers are saying they want, and Caldwell should do his best to make those plans work operationally.

➤ Chris Zook

Chris Zook is a director and the head of worldwide strategy practice at Bain & Company in Boston. He is the author, with James Allen, of Profit from the Core: Growth Strategy in an Era of Turbulence *(Harvard Business School Press, 2001).*

Advaark and GlobalBev are moving dangerously toward mutual value destruction. The ad agency has advised its client to enter the energy drink market late, with inadequate economic justification. And Advaark holds the false hope of an economic bonanza by veering from its core advertising business. Both companies are on the verge of succumbing to what I call the trap of false enthusiasm, wherein a company sees enough of a growth opportunity to be wildly enthusiastic but forgets to ask and insist on answers to the hard questions.

When Bain studied the growth strategies of 2,000 companies worldwide, we found that the most risky decision a company can make is to stray from its core. We've catalogued hundreds of cases of value destruction when companies prematurely abandoned their true strengths. Many sophisticated companies from Sears to Prudential to Zurich Insurance have tried to create bundled offerings to customers, only to return to their cores. Years ago, Saatchi & Saatchi decided to expand its advertising business into IT and management consulting. The result was massive losses and a decade-long strategic reversal. Anheuser-Busch made forays into foods such as Eagle Snacks but discovered (after divesting these businesses) that its beer core, with renewed focus, could grow and be profitable again. And any reader of the business press will hear in GlobalBev's plan echoes of Quaker Oats' disastrous acquisition of Snapple, a decision that destroyed more than $2 billion of shareholder value and absorbed incalculable energy from Quaker's core.

Our research identified five steps that companies can use to judge the real risks and payback of any strategic growth initiative. First, rigorously define the boundaries of your core businesses and get agreement from your management team on the battleground. This is where any growth strategy must begin. Second, decide which cores have the most potential for growth based on their competitive positions and profitability. Ensure that resource allocation favors these cores. Third, determine whether the strongest cores are close to their full growth potential or whether there's more potential to tap. Fourth, map out the opportunities—or "adjacencies"—surrounding the strongest cores. Determine the order in which these opportunities should be addressed, mindful of any relationships among them. Finally, assess whether market leadership is possible in the proposed areas, and evaluate the cost of getting there.

Don't forget that some of the most successful growth strategies are driven by the new needs of core customers. For example, much of the growth of American Express's core card business has come through the meticulous pursuit of "share of wallet" adjacencies to its core customer base. And in broadening its reach through more and more departments of its core customers, Hewlett-Packard has fueled a long growth trajectory for its printer business by increasing the "share of reproductions" from xerography.

Growth always involves taking calculated risks. Companies need to assess the risks and potential outcomes of any new growth initiative while also ensuring that excessive analysis doesn't hinder the speed of decision making. Advaark and GlobalBev need to guard against a decision-making process that resembles too closely the emotionalism of Maygan's ad shoot and too little a calculated quest for successful growth.

Originally published in February 2002

Reprint R0202A

PAUL HEMP

Growing for Broke

Executive Summary

Paragon Tool, a thriving machine tool company in an increasingly tough industry, has been pouring money into growth initiatives. These efforts have shrunk the company's margins, but CEO Nikolas Anaptyxi believes they'll provide the foundation for a profitable future.

Now Paragon is weighing the acquisition of MonitoRobotics, a company with proprietary technology for monitoring the functioning of robotics equipment. The acquisition, which would nearly double Paragon's revenue, could help transform Paragon from a slow-growth manufacturer into a high-growth technology company, bolster its struggling services business, and ultimately allow it to set the standard for how machines communicate with one another. At least, that's what the CEO thinks.

Paragon's CFO, William Littlefield, isn't so sure. He says the move would introduce all the risks that come with acquisitions and put further downward pressure on profits. Paragon's management team is divided, and Anaptyxi must decide how to move forward.

This case study explores growth issues that companies in many industries currently face. The specific dilemma here is, How far should Paragon go in sacrificing profits up front with the aim of generating *real* profits down the line? Commenting on this fictional· case are Rand Araskog, former CEO of ITT; Ken Favaro, CEO of consulting firm Marakon Associates; W. Brian Arthur, an economist known for his work on the idea of increasing returns; and Jay Gellert, CEO of Health Net, a managed-health-care company.

Look, you've *got* to grow. It's what our economy is all about. Hey, it's what our country is all about! Certainly, it's what drives me. My father, Constantine Anaptyxi, came to America from Greece because he saw big opportunities here. He worked hard, took a few risks, and realized his dreams. I came to this company as CEO five years ago—giving up a senior VP position at a *Fortune* 500 manufacturer—because I saw big potential for Paragon Tool, then a small maker of machine tools. I didn't make the move so that I could oversee the company's *down*sizing! I didn't intend to create value—for our customers, for our employees, for our shareholders—by thinking small!! I didn't intend to *shrink* to greatness, for God's sake!!!

Okay, so I'm getting a little worked up over this. Maybe I'm just trying to overcome my own second thoughts about our company's growth plans. I know it isn't just about growth; it's about *profitable* growth, as my CFO, William Littlefield, is always happy to remind me. "Nicky," he'll say, "people always talk about getting to the top when they should be focusing on the bottom . . . line, that is." Quite a comedian, that Littlefield. But lame as the quip is, it tells you a lot about Littlefield and what, in my opinion, is his limited view of business. Sometimes you've got to sacrifice profits up front to make *real* profits down the line.

To me, acquiring MonitoRobotics holds just that kind of promise. The company uses sensor technology and communications software to monitor and report real-time information on the functioning of robotics equipment. By adapting this technology for use on our machine tools, we could offer customers a rapid-response troubleshooting service—what consultants these days like to call a "solutions" business. Over time, I'd hope we could apply the technology and software to other kinds of machine tools and even to other kinds of manufacturing equipment. That would make us less dependent on our slow-growing and cyclical machine-tool manufacturing operation and hopefully give us a strong position in a technology market with terrific growth potential. It would also nearly double our current annual revenue of around $400 million— and force Wall Street to pay some attention to us.

What does Littlefield say to this? Oh, he gives a thumbs-down to the acquisition, of course—too risky. But get this: He also thinks we should sell off our existing services division—a "drag on profits," he says. With the help of some outside consultants, the senior management team has spent the last few months analyzing both our services business and the pros and cons of a MonitoRobotics acquisition. Tomorrow, I need to tell Littlefield whether we should go ahead and put together a presentation on the proposed acquisition for next week's board meeting. If we do move forward on this, I have a hunch a certain CFO might start returning those headhunter calls. And I'd hate to lose him. Whatever our differences, there's no denying that he's capable and smart—in fact, a lot smarter than I am in some areas. On this issue, though, I just don't think he gets it.

Mom and Apple Pie

In 1946, when my father was 21, he left the Greek island of Tinos and came to New York City with his new bride. He worked at a cousin's dry-cleaning store in Astoria, Queens, then started his own on the other side of town. When I was seven, he took his savings and bought a commercial laundry in Brooklyn. Over the next several years, he scooped up one laundry after another, usually borrowing from the bank, sometimes taking another mortgage on the three-family home in Bensonhurst where we had moved. By the time I was a teenager, he was sitting on a million-dollar business that did the linens for all kinds of hotels and hospitals around greater New York. "Nikolas, growth is as American as Mom and apple pie," my father would say to me—he loved using all-American expressions like that. "You gotta get bigger to get better."

My mom was somewhat less expansive in her outlook. She kept my father's accounts, having studied bookkeeping in night school as soon as her English was good enough. And she had her own saying, one that deftly, if inadvertently, bolted together two other platitudes of American slang. "Keep your shirt on," she would say to my father when, arms waving, he would enthusiastically describe some new expansion plan for his business. "Or else you might lose it." My father was the genius behind his company's growth, but I have no doubt that my mother was the one responsible for its profits.

When I was 15, we moved to a nice suburb in Jersey. I never quite fit in: too small for sports, a little too ethnic for the social set, only a middling student. I worked hard, though, and went to Rutgers, where I majored in economics and then stayed on to get an MBA. Something clicked in business school. I seemed to have a knack for solving the real-world problems of the case studies. And I flourished in an environment where the emphasis was on figuring out what you *can* do instead of what you *can't,* on envisioning how things could go right instead of trying to anticipate how they could go wrong. (Thank God I didn't follow my uncle's advice and become a corporate lawyer!)

When I graduated, I got a job at WRT, the Cleveland-based industrial conglomerate where I'd interned the summer before. Over the next 15 years or so, I moved up through the ranks, mainly because of my ability to spot new market opportunities. And by the time I was 45, I was heading up the machine-tool division, a $2.3 billion business. Both revenues and profits surged in the three years I was there, it's true. But I still found my job frustrating. Every proposed acquisition or new initiative of any substance had to be approved by people at headquarters who were far removed from our business. And whenever corporate profits flagged, the response was mindless across-the-board cost cutting that took little account of individual divisions' performance.

So when I was offered the opportunity to head up a small but profitable machine-tool maker in southern Ohio, I jumped at the chance.

Sunflower Tableau

I still remember driving to work my first day at Paragon Tool five years ago. Winding through the Ohio countryside, I saw a stand of sunflowers growing in a rocky patch of soil next to a barn. "Now *there's* a symbol for us," I thought, "a commonplace but hardy plant that quickly grows above its neighbors, often in fairly tough conditions." I was confident that Paragon—a solid, unexceptional business operating in an extremely difficult industry and economic environment—had the potential to grow with similarly glorious results.

For one thing, Paragon was relatively healthy. The company was built around a line of high-end machines—used by manufacturers of aerospace engines, among others—that continued to enjoy fairly good margins, despite the battering that the machine-tool industry as a whole had taken over the previous decade and a half. Still, the market for our product was essentially stagnant. Foreign competition was beginning to take its toll. And we continued to face brutal cyclical economic swings.

I quickly launched a number of initiatives designed to spur revenue growth. With some aggressive pricing, we increased sales and gained share in our core market, driving out a number of our new foreign rivals. We expanded our product line and our customer base by modifying our flagship product for use in a number of other industries. We also made a string of acquisitions in the industrial signage and electronic-labeling field, aiming to leverage the relationships we had with our machine-tool customers. No question, these moves put real pressure on our margins. Along with the price cuts and the debt we took on to make the acquisitions, we had to invest in new manufacturing equipment and a larger sales force. But we were laying the foundation for what I hoped would be a highly profitable future. The board and the senior management team, including Littlefield, seemed to share my view.

Indeed, the CFO and I had developed a rapport, despite our differing business instincts. Early on in our working relationship, this sixth-generation Yankee started in with the kidding about my alma mater. "Is that how they taught you to think about it at Rutgers?" he'd say if I was brainstorming and came up with some crazy idea. "Because at *Wharton*, they taught us . . ." I'd just laugh and then tell whoever else was in the room how proud we were that Littlefield had been a cheerleader for the Penn football team—like that was his biggest scholarly accomplishment. One time he "let it slip" that in fact he was Phi Beta Kappa, and we all just groaned. I said, "Give it up, Littlefield. You may have been Phi Beta Kappa, but, despite those letters on your gold pin, you'll never out-*Greek* me." To tell the truth, our skills are complementary, and between us we manage to do a pretty good job for the company.

As Paragon grew, so did the sense of excitement and urgency among our managers—indeed, among the entire workforce. People who once had been merely con-

---

As Paragon grew, so did the sense of excitement and urgency among our managers—indeed, among the entire workforce.

---

tent to work at Paragon now couldn't wait to tackle the next challenge. And that excitement spread throughout the small Ohio town where we are based. When I'd go with my wife to a party or speak at the local Rotary Club or even stop to buy gas, people would show a genuine interest in the company and our latest doings—it helped that we always mentioned the job-creation impact when announcing new initiatives. There's no doubt it stoked my ego to be one of the bigger fish in the local pond. But even more important for me was the sense that this was business at its best, providing people with a justified sense of well-being about the present and confidence in the future.

Anyway, my point here is that we've grown fast since I arrived, but we still have a long way to go. I've come to think that the real key to our future is in the company's services division. We currently offer our customers the option to buy a standard service contract, under which we provide periodic machine maintenance and respond to service calls. But we've been developing technology and software, similar to MonitoRobotics', that would allow us to respond immediately if a machine at a customer's site goes down. The division currently accounts for less than 10% of our revenue and, because of the cost of developing the new technology, it's struggling to turn a profit.

But I can see in the services division the seeds of a business that will ultimately transform us from a manufacturing company into a high-tech company. Such a transformation, requiring an overhaul of our culture and capabilities, won't be easy. And it will surely require significant additional investments. But the potential upside is huge, with the promise of sales and profit growth that could make our current single-digit gains seem trivial by comparison. Besides, what choice do we have? A number of our competitors have already spotted these opportunities and have begun moving ahead with them. If we don't ramp up quickly, we might well miss out on the action altogether.

A Company in Play

Just over a month ago, I was sitting at my desk preparing a presentation for the handful of analysts who cover our company. Until recently, most of them have had only good things to say about all our growth moves. But last quarter, when we again reported a year-on-year drop in earnings, a few of them started asking pointed questions about our investments and when they could be expected to bear fruit. As I was giving some thought to how I'd answer their questions in the upcoming meeting, the phone rang. It was our investment banker, Jed Nixon.

"Nicky, I think we should talk," he said. I could tell from the sound of his voice he was on to something big, and then he told me what it was: "MonitoRobotics is in play."

We both did some calendar juggling and managed to get together for lunch the very next day at Jed's office in Cincinnati. The rumor was that one of our direct competitors, Bellows & Samson, was about to launch a hostile takeover bid for MonitoRobotics. As it happened, we had just started a conversation with MonitoRobotics' management a few months before, about collaborating on remote servicing technology for machine tools. But Jed's call had had its intended effect, changing my thinking about the company: Why not acquire it ourselves?

Although MonitoRobotics' technology was designed to detect and report operating failures in robotics equipment, managers there had told us when we met that adapting it for use on other industrial machinery was feasible. Indeed, MonitoRobotics had recently licensed the technology to a company that planned to modify it for use on complex assembly lines that experienced frequent breakdowns. Our engineers had confirmed that a version could be developed for our machines—though in their initial assessment they hadn't been exactly sure how long this would take.

Still, the potential benefits of acquiring MonitoRobotics seemed numerous. It would give us a powerful presence in a fast-growing business while preempting a competitor from staking a claim there. Whatever the time lag in adapting MonitoRobotics' technology for use with our products, we would almost certainly be able to offer our customers this valuable troubleshooting service more quickly than if we continued to develop the technology ourselves. And though our products were different, MonitoRobotics and Paragon potentially served many of the same manufacturing customers. "Think of the cross-selling opportunities," Jed said, as he took a bite of his sandwich. The greatest opportunity, though, lay in the possibility that Monito-Robotics' software technology would become the standard means for machine tools—and ultimately a variety of industrial machines—to communicate their service needs to the people who serviced them and to other machines that might be affected by their shutdown.

This was a fairly speculative train of thought. But a MonitoRobotics acquisition had for me the earmarks of a breakthrough opportunity for Paragon. And our earlier conversations with its management team had been cordial, suggesting the company might welcome a friendly offer from us to counter Bellows & Samson's hostile bid. Of course, even if we were able to get MonitoRobotics at a fair price, an acquisition of this size would further delay our return to the margins and profit growth we had known in the past. And that, I knew, wouldn't sit well with everyone.

Management Dissension

The day after my meeting with Jed, I called together members of our senior management team. There was a barely suppressed gasp when I mentioned the potential acquisition, particularly given its size. "Boy, that would be a lot to digest with everything we've got on our plate right now," said Joe McCollum, our senior VP of marketing. "It also might represent the chance of a lifetime," countered Rosemary Witkowski, head of the services division. Then Littlefield spoke up. His skepticism wasn't surprising.

"I was just running a few simple numbers on what the MonitoRobotics acquisition might mean to our bottom line," he said. "Besides the costs associated with the acquisition itself, we'd be looking at some significant expenses in the near term, including accelerated software research, hiring and training, and even brand development." He pointed out that these costs would put further pressure on our earnings, just as our profits were struggling to recover from earlier growth-related investments.

Littlefield did concede that a bold acquisition like this might be just the sort of growth move that would appeal to some of our analysts—and might even prompt a few more securities firms to cover us. But he insisted that if our earnings didn't start bouncing back soon, Wall Street was going to pillory us. Then he dropped his bombshell: "I frankly think this is an opportunity to consider getting out of the services business altogether. Eliminating the continued losses that we've been experiencing there would allow us to begin realizing the profit growth that we can expect from the investments we've made in our still-healthy machine-tool business."

Littlefield argued that, whether we acquired MonitoRobotics or not, it wasn't clear we'd be able to dominate the machine-tool services market because a number of our competitors were already flocking there. Furthermore, the market might not be worth fighting over: Many of our customers were struggling with profitability themselves and might not be willing or able to buy our add-on services. "Last one in, turn out the lights" was the phrase Littlefield used to describe the rush to dominate a profitless market.

As soon as she had a chance, Rosemary shot back in defense of her operation. "This is the one area we're in that has significant growth potential," she said. "And we've already sunk an incredible amount of money into developing this software. I can't believe you'd throw all of that investment out the window." But a number of heads nodded when Littlefield argued that we'd recoup much of that investment if we sold the money-losing business.

Several days later, I polled the members of the senior management team and found them split on the issue of the acquisition. And, to be honest, I was beginning to doubt myself on this. I respected Littlefield's financial savvy. And no one had yet raised the issue of whether Paragon, a traditional manufacturing company, had the management capabilities to run what was essentially a software start-up. We decided to hire two highly regarded consulting firms to do quick analyses of the proposed MonitoRobotics acquisition.

The Sunflowers' Successor

Today, the consultants came back to us with conflicting reports. One highlighted the market potential of MonitoRobotics' technology, noting that we might be too far behind to develop similar technology on our own. The other focused on the difficulties both of integrating the company's technology with ours and of adapting it to equipment beyond the robotics field.

So as I drove home tonight, the dilemma seemed no closer to being resolved. In many ways, I am persuaded by the cautionary message of Littlefield's number crunching. At the same time, I firmly believe the pros and cons of such a complex decision can't be precisely quantified; sometimes you just have to go with your instincts—which in my case favor growth. As I turned the issue over in my head, I looked out the car window, half-consciously seeking inspired insight. Sure enough, there was the barn where the sunflowers had been growing five years before. But the bright yellow blossoms, highlighted by the red timbers of the barn, were gone. Instead, a carpet of green kudzu was growing up the side of the increasingly dilapidated building. This fast-growing vine, which already had ravaged much of the South, was now spreading, uncontrolled and unproductive, into southern Ohio.

My mind started to drift and the image of kudzu—a more sinister symbol of growth than the sunflower—began to merge with thoughts of my father, who had died of lung cancer two years before, and my mother, who these days spends most of her time managing her investments. Suddenly, my parents' favorite phrases came to mind. It occurred to me that kudzu was now becoming as American as Mom and apple pie. Even so, its dense foliage certainly seemed like a place where, if you weren't careful, you could easily misplace your shirt.

Should Paragon Tool Further Its Growth Ambitions by Trying to Acquire MonitoRobotics?

Four commentators offer expert advice.

➤ Rand Araskog

Rand Araskog was the chief executive officer of ITT Corporation from 1979 through 1998. He is the author of The ITT Wars: A CEO Speaks Out on Takeovers *(Henry Holt, 1989).*

Nicky Anaptyxi becomes too pessimistic as he drives home at the end of the story. When you have a unique acquisition opportunity, which MonitoRobotics would seem to represent, you have to move on it, even if it results in a short-term hit to profitability. You can't spend too much time worrying about things—apart from the crucial issue of how much to pay—especially if a competing bidder is waiting in the wings.

You might think that I'd be a skeptic of acquisition-driven growth because of my experience at ITT, both working with Harold Geneen to build that quintessential conglomerate in the 1960s and 1970s and then, as CEO, separating ITT into independent, publicly traded companies. But there's nothing wrong with acquisitions. We continued to make acquisitions in the 1980s and 1990s to fortify ITT's various business segments. By the mid-1990s, it simply became clear that the company's growth potential—and value to shareholders—would be enhanced if it were broken into separate entities, each with a clear business focus.

For Paragon Tool, the acquisition seems to have such focus and could thus strengthen the company's competitive position in a market with lots of growth potential. If you sell reasonably complicated equipment, you should be the one to service it. And there's money to be made in doing that; just ask United Technologies about the relative profitability of making Otis elevators and servicing them. In the case of Paragon, the services business, even if not yet profitable, shows the most potential for profitable growth, whether organically or through acquisitions.

The question of which way to grow the services business highlights Nicky's real dilemma: How much should Paragon pay for MonitoRobotics? With a rival also interested, the company needs to quickly figure out the right price and do a deal before a bidding war commences. If the price becomes too high, though, the company must be willing to walk away from the acquisition and continue to build its services business internally.

The need to determine the right price presents an opportunity for Nicky to engage, and ultimately hold on to, his talented CFO. No matter how brilliant Littlefield may be, he is no good to Paragon if he and Nicky don't operate as a team. They can do this by complementing and counterbalancing one another—for instance, Nicky as the gung-ho cavalry charger and Littlefield as the cautious fort holder. But they can't be at odds. Nicky must make clear that the services division represents the future of the business. If Littlefield doesn't agree, Nicky needs to hire a new CFO.

Meanwhile, Nicky can at least get Littlefield involved by appealing to his strengths and assigning him the task of determining a fair price for MonitoRobotics. While Nicky and the board might ultimately decide, for strategic reasons, that the CFO's recommended offer price is too low—for example, they may be willing to accept a dilution in earnings for a year or two—Littlefield's conservative perspective will still be useful. Indeed, his analysis may convince them that it would in the end make more financial sense for the company to focus on developing its own services technology. On the other hand, Littlefield might find in the course of his analysis that the deal does seem like the right move for the company.

There is one final thing Nicky needs to consider: his own character. He's clearly a hard-driving builder who wouldn't be happy—or successful—reconstructing a slimmed-down company. What might arguably be a viable strategy for Paragon—downsizing to increase profitability—isn't viable if he is the one charged with executing it.

That's why it is a mistake for Nicky to suddenly get discouraged at the end. He forgets—or perhaps doesn't know—that in season kudzu blooms with clusters of stunning reddish-purple flowers. He shouldn't let his current emotional trough obscure the potential beauty of this acquisition.

➤ Ken Favaro

Ken Favaro is the chief executive of Marakon Associates, an international strategy-consulting firm based in New York.

Years of research on acquisitions point to the same conclusion: Up to 75% of them fail to create value for shareholders. When you take that into account, Littlefield's opposition to acquiring MonitoRobotics seems to make sense. And yet, a recent study by our firm of the most successful value-creating companies found that many of them have, in fact, been acquisitive. In many markets, up to 50% of these companies have grown *primarily* through acquisition. Given this conflicting evidence, how is Nikolas to decide whether the acquisition would be a wise move?

The first thing he needs to do is stop viewing the potential acquisition in isolation and ask himself, "What are our growth alternatives?" Nikolas seems to focus on the question of *whether* to grow rather than *how* to grow. For example, when challenged by Littlefield, Nikolas engages in an unhelpful debate that focuses on the false dichotomy between short-term profit and long-term growth. In my experience, the only established companies forced to trade off near-term profits for top-line growth are those with broken business models. And if a company's business model is broken, management should focus on fixing it and making it profitable before worrying about growth.

Nikolas's failure to consider alternative paths to growth runs two important risks. First, if acquiring MonitoRobotics is the only alternative considered, then failing to acquire the company will leave Paragon without a growth strategy, potentially backing Nikolas and the company's board into a corner. Since it is human nature to choose action over inaction—in this case, some growth strategy over no growth strategy—the deal will likely go through, no matter what the cost.

Second, by not considering alternatives, Nikolas may be overlooking better ways to grow. The services business may be the wrong growth vehicle. After all, as Littlefield points out, it hasn't been profitable, and the machine-tool services market—despite the positive aura that surrounds the concept of services these days—may well end up being profitless for all participants. Managers should be wary of plans to generate growth in unprofitable businesses, particularly when the rationale for doing so is grounded in a fear that, as Nicky puts it, you'll "miss out on the action." Venture capitalists have for years applied a "three years to profitability or out" test to their investments; corporations would be wise to consider a similar standard. While it may be time for Paragon to double its bet on its services division, it may also be time to fold and play a different hand. Nikolas and the board won't know unless Paragon explicitly examines alternative growth strategies.

In addition to the risks presented by Nikolas's failure to consider alternatives, there is the more basic question of whether acquiring MonitoRobotics is a smart move. For an acquisition to have a reasonable shot at generating value growth, it must meet three important criteria: a good fit, the right price, and excellent execution. At this point, Nikolas doesn't know enough about fit to make a call one way or the other. He knows nothing about price. And one can't help but sense that there will be real problems with execution. Nikolas has already acknowledged that the transformation of Paragon from a manufacturing company into a technology company will require an overhaul of its culture and capabilities. Without the support of his team and complete agreement on how best to generate growth, it is highly unlikely that Paragon's management will execute the MonitoRobotics acquisition effectively—even if the fit and price are right.

So my advice to Nikolas? Stop, take a deep breath—and then take three months to get the top team, and ultimately the board, to agree on whether acquiring MonitoRobotics is the best alternative for growing the company. If the answer is yes, the team will have reached consensus around fit and price, making excellent execution much more likely. If, on the other hand, the answer is no, then Paragon will have dodged a big bullet.

➤ W. Brian Arthur

W. Brian Arthur is the Citibank Professor at the Santa Fe Institute in New Mexico. From 1983 to 1996, he was the Morrison Professor of Economics and Population Studies at Stanford University in California. He is the author of "Increasing Returns and the New World of Business" (HBR July–August 1996).

The acquisition is an obvious go. If a company doesn't keep developing and renewing itself, it can easily lose momentum and, eventually, its competitive edge. And MonitoRobotics seems to offer Paragon reasonable prospects for development, especially if its technology can be adapted for use with other classes of machinery—not just those of Paragon and its rivals.

But let me offer a few caveats. First, this doesn't seem to be a case about growth but rather about repositioning. The acquisition would allow Paragon to build a new skill base and enter new markets, not simply grow within its existing set of capabilities and industry. And if you're going to reposition yourself like this as a way to create a new platform for future revenue, you almost inevitably have to accept some temporary losses. Littlefield's observation about profitable growth suggests that he doesn't understand this.

Indeed, the CFO's comments highlight the fact that Nicky faces not just a business problem but also a political one: If the acquisition represents a sensible repositioning of the company, he needs to build consensus among his executives, his board, and his shareholders. Of course, he may not be able to convince every one of his colleagues. If Little-field continues to object to the acquisition, most likely he will start to make trouble later. In that case, the CEO should encourage him to walk.

Let me just add a quick observation about Paragon's move into what it calls services. In this case, services actually means servic*ing*—that is, the fairly routine business of troubleshooting and maintenance. But as fail-safe mechanisms increasingly are designed into complicated machinery, many servicing capabilities become redundant. It is ironic that for Paragon to gain market share in its main manufacturing business, it will have to make machine tools that are increasingly trouble-free—and such reliability may ultimately drive its nascent service arm out of business.

Despite that conflict, MonitoRobotics does create longer-term opportunities for Paragon. And these involve more sophisticated forms of monitoring and repair. MonitoRobotics' current technology merely accelerates Paragon's existing servicing process. Instead of a line worker reporting a problem to a foreman, who then calls a repairman, the company's sensors detect a problem and immediately inform the manufacturer, who sends technicians to fix it.

But this technology is only the first step toward machines that monitor themselves, that detect deviations and variations in tolerance and then automatically correct those problems as they continue to operate. This self-correction might require a digital link with the manufacturer, which could then automatically send adjustment specifications back to the machine through phone link or satellite.

This sounds futuristic, but it's a natural set of activities for MonitoRobotics to move into. And it applies to *all* machines, not just those of Paragon and its competitors. So the acquisition has rich possibilities for future expansion.

The new combined company will be more high-tech than before. But will its technology allow it to dominate its market through network effects and the creation of a new standard? I don't think so. Even if Paragon's technology becomes widespread, it will not establish a "language" that other machines will have to speak. But the acquisition will establish a new skill base—a capability that Paragon can use to build on.

➤ Jay Gellert

Jay Gellert is the CEO of Health Net, one of the nation's largest publicly traded managed-health-care companies, based in Woodland Hills, California.

This case certainly provides a model for the wrong way to go about assessing a deal, especially in today's environment. Indeed, Paragon seems to be taking a "very '90s" approach. I speak with some authority here: One element of our company's turnaround in the past two-and-a-half years has been the divestment of several businesses acquired during our rapid expansion over the previous decade.

Start with the fact that Paragon doesn't appear to have in place a well-thought-out approach to growth. Now, you may do a deal because your own prospects are weak, and you realize that risky acquisitions are the only hope of avoiding an even riskier future—the classic case of one drunken man looking for another to hold him up. Or you may do a deal because you are in a strong position and acquisitions will allow you to pump more offerings through a healthy product and distribution infrastructure. You might even do a deal because you have determined it would be catastrophic if someone else beat you to it.

But you need a clear reason to make the acquisition. There is a kind of meandering quality to Paragon's approach that borrows a bit of reasoning from each of the preceding scenarios. Indeed, the company's interest in acquiring MonitoRobotics is primarily reactive: When the two companies were talking about a possible joint venture, before the rumors of a hostile bid, an acquisition wasn't even considered. Certainly, there are times when you need to do something to match a competitor's move, but if that is the sole reason for an acquisition, it's almost guaranteed to fail. Paragon's hazily defined approach to growth is highlighted by the management schism that has occurred. The differences between the CEO and CFO on the company's direction should have been confronted long before a specific deal was even contemplated.

The potential acquisition raises a number of other red flags. It is portrayed almost entirely as what I call a "strategic deal"—that is, the financial benefits will only be realized far in the future or can't be quantified at all. You get the strong sense that the acquisition would seriously stretch Paragon's financial resources and that a lot of things have to go right in order for it to work. Again, such an acquisition may be justified if it is part of a cohesive growth plan. But this has that random-amalgamation feel that characterized many acquisitions in the 1990s.

Even more worrisome, the acquisition is billed as one that will transform the company—always a risky proposition, given the immediate change in culture that this requires. The management team appears clueless as to how it will manage this change and other aspects of integrating MonitoRobotics, whose main asset as a services business is its people. Such a transformative acquisition is doubly dangerous when done defensively, in reaction to a rival's move.

The company also needs to think about how shareholders and analysts will respond. While they might have been enthusiastic about such an acquisition five years ago, they are unlikely to welcome it today. For one thing, there is less tolerance for revenue as a mere forerunner of profits. Concerns that a company isn't moving fast enough have been replaced by fears that it doesn't appreciate the execution challenges of a merger. People also demand greater line-of-sight linkage between an acquisition and its benefits; big-concept moves—"this transforms us into a technology company"—are met with more skepticism. And in these post-Enron days, the departure of a respected and conservative CFO over such a deal would set off alarm bells.

This might have been a brilliant acquisition for Paragon four years ago. Back then, many companies might have done such a deal. But times have changed. Realizing the potential perils of such acquisitions has made our management team and board much more disciplined in our thinking about them. Paragon should apply the same rigor.

Originally published in September 2002

Reprint R0209A

Cross Selling or

Cross Purposes?

Executive Summary

Software maker TopTek has acquired a consulting and systems-integration firm, mainly to profit from the software sales that are a natural by-product of consulting engagements. But in many ways the two companies worked better when they were separate.

Before the acquisition, the consulting firm's sales were made by the same people who delivered services to clients. TopTek's sales, by contrast, were handled by the company's professional salespeople, all of them highly skilled at selling product. Now the consultants and the salespeople are trying to work together, but they're making a hash of it.

For instance, the CIO of a TopTek customer—a retailer—is complaining that consultants from the acquired firm are driving him nuts. They've got his boss's ear, and they're selling additional projects left and right, stimulating demand for a pace of change that the CIO says the retailer can't handle.

The consultants in newly constituted TopTek aren't happy either. They get no commissions on products they sell, because commissions for all sales to an account—forever—go to the salesperson who snagged it in the first place.

The sales force has its own gripes. The consultants aren't much help in winning new business, according to Ron Murphy, TopTek's sales VP. "Most of them couldn't sell sunscreen at a nudist colony," he says.

What will it take for cross selling to succeed at TopTek? Commenting on this fictional case study are Ram Charan, an author and advisor to CEOs; Caroline A. Kovac, the general manager of IBM Healthcare and Life Sciences; Jerome A. Colletti, an author and consultant; and Federico Turegano, the managing director of SG Corporate and Investment Banking, an arm of Société Générale Group.

"How was your weekend?" John asked.

"Just fine. We got away to the lake."

"Hey, that's right—you have a place up there. How long have you had it now?"

This was John's standard way of getting to what was on his mind. Anna decided to cut directly to the heart of the matter. "About three years. So what's up, John?"

Anna Tucker was officially the vice president for human resources at TopTek, maker of software for middle-market companies, but no more than half her time was devoted to HR. The rest, the fun part, was spent as CEO John Vaunt's troubleshooter. He gave her all of the problems that didn't fit neatly anywhere else and those he didn't want messed up.

"We had dinner with Ric Gudalskis and his wife on Saturday," John began. "Do you know Ric? He's CIO at DigiDeal Stores, which has been a good account. He said he thought I should know something: Since the acquisition, we've been driving him nuts. Our people are in there trying to sell additional projects left and right. Ric feels we're churning the pot, trying to stimulate demand for a pace of change that the company can't handle, and taking up too much of management's time while we're at it. I called Peter Lee on Sunday to ask him about it, and he gave me an earful. I don't want to bias you—you should hear it from Peter yourself—but I think our sales compensation structure may be broken."

"That could be part of the problem," Anna offered cautiously.

"Whatever it is, would you look into it? With the sale of product flattening out, we need to sell more services; that's where the growth is. But we can't abuse our customers in the process."

Sins of Commission

Nine months earlier, TopTek had acquired the systems-integration and consulting firm Rossberg Lee, which had been one of TopTek's alliance partners. Both parties had stood to gain from the marriage. TopTek hoped to snag more of the software sales that were a natural by-product of a Rossberg Lee consulting engagement. And Peter Lee, the former head of Rossberg Lee and now executive vice president of the Solutions division at TopTek, was excited about TopTek's foot in the door at a much broader range of companies. The newly merged organization had spent a lot of time developing "solutions"—standard bundles of products and services to take to market. More customized and expensive offerings were also available.

But in many ways the two organizations had worked better as partners than as parts of the same company. Anna knew that John Vaunt's concern about the consultants was only the latest sign of friction. So when she met with Peter later that day, she wasn't surprised to get an earful herself.

Peter paced the floor of his office while they talked. It was clear that he had been stung by John's query. "Gudalskis isn't really concerned about all those calls

---

"Frankly, the sales force only knows how to push product. Selling a solution designed to meet a client need takes a consultant's perspective."

---

to his people," he said defensively. "He just doesn't like the fact that I play golf with his boss. CIOs don't like it when consultants have better access than they do." Anna couldn't help glancing toward the corner of Peter's office, where a display case housed several ornate golf trophies. "John should recognize that it's my relationship with Gudalskis's boss that got us that new work last month. I'm talking about the HR package they signed up for. The account manager had nothing to do with it—though, of course, that won't stop him from collecting his commission."

"So we don't need a sales force?" Anna asked, knowing Peter could take a gentle jabbing.

"The sales force is great at getting us into new accounts. But once a company has signed up for the basic financial package, they don't have the technical knowledge or the day-to-day contact that will lead to add-on business. Ed Forsythe practically camped out at DigiDeal for the final month of the rollout of the basic package," Peter said, referring to the principal consultant on the engagement. "I was there a lot myself. That's how you get the ties that bind. And it's how your consultants get to really understand a client's business. Frankly, the sales force only knows how to push product. Selling a solution designed to meet a client need takes a consultant's perspective."

"OK," Anna said, sighing, "but we can't just leave it at that. Otherwise, what was the point of our combining forces?" She took a breath and forged ahead. "Peter, you just made a remark about a commission. Is there something out of whack about our incentives?"

"Well, think about it," Peter said with a scowl. "The current compensation structure rewards the sales force for all the work sold into an account forever, regardless of whether they contributed to the sale. Our people—the consultants in Solutions—have to sell to keep billable, but the commissions go to the salespeople who won the accounts, even if it was years ago. Does a structure like that make any sense?"

"The salespeople's contributions are important, though," Anna said.

"Of course they are. Sometimes. But there are big holes." Peter glanced toward the door, where his assistant was mouthing a name and indicating a telephone with her thumb and pinky. "Excuse me," he said, striding toward his desk. "That's a call from a client that I just have to take. But I'll tell you who you should talk to: Lelia Chase. She's a Solutions person who calls into accounts directly—just what Gudalskis was complaining about."

Sins of Omission

Lelia was in charge of the consulting practice that implemented the facilities package of TopTek's major product suite. Anna welcomed the chance to talk with her. Lelia was professional and coolheaded; she could be counted on to be objective. Still, it was a strange recommendation. Implementations of this assemblage of software and services for customers' facilities management functions accounted for a small fraction of the company's revenue. Few customers signed up for it.

The two arranged to meet in the company cafeteria, which had been upgraded since the merger and now served gourmet meals that were worth staying on campus for. Lelia picked at her Caesar salad. "So, you've been asked to look at the way work is sold and rewards are given out. My condolences," she said. "You're a sucker for all the choice assignments, aren't you?" This was Lelia's way of acknowledging Anna's role as troubleshooter. Anna found it flattering.

"Why do you think Peter asked me to talk with you?" Anna asked.

"Because if I waited for the sales force to sell work for us, our practice would starve."

Anna, in the middle of a bite, could only register a surprised expression. Lelia elaborated. "The price of a facilities implementation is about a quarter of the price of any other package. Our projects are tiny. But it's going to take the account rep just as much time to sell work for us as it would to sell any other package. He has to build relationships with people in the client's facilities department—people he has no other reason to get to know. He'd much rather be selling a juicy financial, HR, or sales package instead."

"So *you* have to sell it."

"Right. I don't blame them for being uninterested. But I can't wait around. I won't be able to hang on to the team I've built up over the past five years if I can't keep them busy. None of us will get our bonuses if we don't reach our utilization targets. So I sell."

"I sense you'd rather not."

Lelia shrugged. "I don't mind. Besides, I have some advantages over the account reps. I deal with facilities people every day and understand their problems. I belong to the right associations. The account reps don't really understand what we do. There are several small units in Rossberg Lee—excuse me, I mean in Solutions—that suffer from this problem. I've asked if the company is really interested in our practice areas and I'm told that it is, that we are needed so the firm can offer a competitive array of products and services."

Anna brought up the question of commissions, asking if it bothered Lelia that account reps got a cut of the work she sold.

There was a long pause. "I don't understand it," Lelia said. "But I figure the higher-ups have their reasons."

She doesn't want to alienate the account reps, Anna thought, but the system seems crazy to her.

Lelia continued: "In this market, facilities software isn't all that popular with clients. But when companies are growing, there's a lot of interest. I have to keep us going until the market turns and interest heats up again. Then, I suspect, the sales force will notice us.

"The funny thing is that before the merger, I was always considered a hero for going out and selling my own work. Now it upsets people."

The Princes of Sales

Anna needed to hear the sales organization's point of view. Ron Murphy, vice president of sales and marketing, showed up for the meeting with a face almost as red as his tie.

"You'd think I'd have learned by my age," he said with a laugh. "But it was such a beautiful weekend, and one of our customers invited us out on his boat. I should have taken a hat." He laughed again. "So what's this about changing the compensation formula for sales?"

Anna knew better than to take Ron's easy manner at face value. TopTek owed a lot of its success to his relentless drive. She described what she had learned about the DigiDeal case.

"I've known Peter for ten years, and I'm a big supporter of his," Ron said. "He's one of the smartest guys I know, and, as you're aware, I pushed the acquisition of his firm. But he doesn't understand sales."

"I think Peter's a pretty good salesman, based on his record," Anna said.

"Sure he is. One of the best. It's because of Peter and one or two others that we bought Rossberg Lee. I mean he doesn't understand what it takes to manage a sales force. For all Peter's posturing, Solutions sales are only 20% of the business. If we're going to make our numbers, we need hard-driving salespeople who are amply rewarded for their efforts. The Solutions camp can't deliver the goods. Aside from Peter and a few others, most of them feel selling is unprofessional. They don't want to dirty their hands.

"Albert Washington worked for three years to get us into DigiDeal. The basic financial package they bought was smaller than usual. So if Al had been compensated for that package and that package alone, he wouldn't have had much to show for his hard work, would he? And now, his account is generating all kinds of revenue for TopTek. Peter and his consultants wouldn't even know DigiDeal existed if it weren't for Al. I don't question the job that Peter Lee and Ed Forsythe did there, but you can't screw Al out of his commission on last month's HR implementation. He wouldn't stay if all he got was a commission on the initial package."

Anna could recall at least two other occasions when she had been threatened with the loss of Prince Albert. "Yes," she said, "but if he didn't really contribute to the sale—"

"You have to understand how sales works. Sometimes you work your butt off, do everything right, and you still don't win. Sometimes it comes too easy. It all nets out. Al spends his time where it's needed. He senses things are going well at DigiDeal, so he devotes more time to Southland Baking, which, by the way, is about to sign up for an HR and a planning implementation this month. You want to penalize him for doing the right thing? Ed Forsythe is the project principal on that account, too. You think he worked hard on it? He was too busy at DigiDeal to be bothered with Southland. But Al knows you have to stay in front of your customers."

"Peter said Ed practically lived at DigiDeal for a month to help with that rollout."

"Look, the consultants get compensated, and *well* compensated, on utilization. They didn't do much to sell the extension work at Southland, but they'll still get rewarded for the work they do there. They want it both ways."

"How much of the first sale at DigiDeal was product and how much was services?" Anna asked.

"I can tell you've been talking to Peter. He's always accusing our people of 'pushing products rather than crafting solutions'—nothing pejorative about that language, is there? But he's got a point. If you want to do something helpful, find out how to train account reps to sell solutions. And while you're at it, train Peter's consultants to sell anything at all. At least my guys can sell product. Most of the consultants couldn't sell sunscreen at a nudist colony."

Anna laughed, in spite of herself. The idea of some of Rossberg Lee's more introverted techies in that kind of situation was amusing, she had to admit.

Searching for What Works

At the cabin by the lake that weekend, Anna found her thoughts turning continually to the conversations she'd been having. On Saturday evening, during a walk along the water's edge, her husband noticed she was preoccupied. "What's wrong?" he asked.

She tried to explain, though she knew he often found her business life mystifying. "Maybe the merger just isn't working," he ventured.

Maybe it's not, she thought as she watched the fireflies in the gathering darkness. But no, the logic behind it still held up. Sales and consulting each had its own inimitable way of getting businesses to open their wallets. And if they helped each other, the company would get a bigger share of wallet than it could hope to if they worked independently. It certainly seemed to be working that way at the Trigestis Pharmaceuticals account, the success story being touted by TopTek to the financial analysts. Maybe she could find the answers there.

A Productive Pairing

On Monday afternoon, she met with Tricia Bolling, a project partner from Solutions, and Charlie Hoaver, the account executive assigned to Trigestis. Anna explained her mission. "You two have succeeded wildly at Trigestis. Has the compensation system for rewarding sales helped or hurt?"

"I try not to think about that," joked Tricia. "If I did, it might just break up our team."

Anna laughed. "Do you agree with that, Charlie?"

"Well, I never saw a sales compensation system that worked perfectly. This one's OK, I guess."

"So how do we create more successes like Trigestis?"

"Hire more account execs like Charlie," said Tricia.

"Could you elaborate on that a little?"

"Yeah, I'd like to hear more about that, too," Charlie said.

"I can trust him," Tricia said. "Just after the merger, I took an account rep, who will remain nameless, to meet with the president of one of my old accounts. We were there to explain why the two firms had joined up and to reassure him that it would enhance the relationship we had with his company. The client was gracious, and the meeting went along fine, until he indirectly mentioned a need he had. The account rep pounced on it, saying how much we would like to help him with it. He even brought out a brochure. It was totally inappropriate, and my client gave me a look I still remember. He hadn't agreed to a sales meeting, and we were out of there two minutes later. I had to call him up and apologize.

"Charlie would never make a mistake like that. He knows how to listen to accounts and when to come to me and my consultants and ask us to support him. Meanwhile, he's out there in the marketplace, which I don't have the time to be. We've sold more services and product at Trigestis than at any other account of its size as a result. Watch us do the same thing at the other companies we've targeted."

"Keep talking. I'm loving this," Charlie said. "Seriously, I could say the same thing about Tricia. I trust her. If I spend six months getting a customer to the point where he wants a meeting, I can trust her not to cancel on short notice because a current customer asked for the same time slot. When I introduce her to someone, she doesn't go on about the latest technical fix till their eyes glaze over instead of listening to their problem. And she doesn't drop the ball."

Impressive, thought Anna as she left them, but how do we replicate that?

Overhaul or Tweak?

"Well, Anna, what have you found?" asked John.

"We're hung up on a number of dimensions," she responded. "Our sales force provides broad market coverage and our consultants provide content knowledge and deep working relationships. We need both, but we don't yet have a way to sort out the two of them."

"Compensation can clarify different people's priorities," John observed.

"Yes, but there are other issues as well. In many ways, the legacy TopTek and legacy Rossberg Lee people were better suited to their old organizations than to one that sells solutions. We are going to need to start recruiting to some new job profiles."

"I understand that, but even if I wanted to, I couldn't turn over a majority of the workforce in the next year without causing more problems than I solve. And I need results before then."

What Will It Take for Cross Selling
to Succeed at TopTek?

Four commentators offer expert advice.

➤ Ram Charan

*Ram Charan (office@charanassoc.com) is an adviser to CEOs,
an expert in corporate governance, and an author and coauthor whose books include* Profitable Growth Is Everyone's
Business: 10 Tools You Can Use Monday Morning *(Crown Business, 2004) and* Execution *(Crown Business, 2002). His book*
Confronting Reality *is forthcoming from Crown Business.*

What makes this case especially interesting to me is the CEO's blind spot. Evidently he's a good growth strategist; the acquisition of the consulting partner Rossberg Lee made sense, and the company was correct to focus immediately on crafting full-fledged solutions for customers. But John Vaunt is now falling into the trap that catches so many CEOs when they are too hands-off—looking to the compensation system to get the job done.

Pay for performance is always important, and always tricky to get right in sales organizations, but a lack of proper incentives hasn't been to blame in companies where I've seen cross selling efforts founder. Instead, problems tend to arise from three other challenges.

First, there's the difficulty of creating a coherent offering. Customers will buy bundled products and services only if it is evident to them that they're getting more value from the bundle than they'd get if they bought the components separately. But many vendors approach the problem inside out, slapping products together in ways that make life easier for the vendors rather than the customers. Using a term like "cross selling" doesn't help—in fact, the phrase should be banned in any company hoping to do more business with existing customers.

The second challenge is defining a distinct set of customers and working backward to design a solution from their perspective—understanding how they will experience it, using their language, and incorporating their priorities. This is an exercise in segmentation and looking at the company's offerings from the outside. TopTek hasn't engaged in this exercise.

And, finally, there is the training challenge presented by a new and more sophisticated type of offering. The company must cultivate new skills in salespeople, and across selling teams, to enable the sales force to understand the decision process in the customer's shop, identify the critical decision makers, and speak to those key people in their language.

Classroom training probably wouldn't be effective. Because of the mix of skills involved in solutions selling, there are not many trainers who can teach it. TopTek would do better to adopt an apprenticeship model, with trainees learning from people who are already experts. Of course, the time of those top salespeople is extremely valuable, so the training format must make efficient use of it. Charlie and Tricia, for example, could reasonably be asked to train ten salespeople via e-learning or conference calls. An hour every day—or even once a week—would produce results. One question is whether Ron Murphy, TopTek's VP of sales and marketing, is skilled enough to be one of the trainers. If he isn't, it will be hard for him to identify, hire, and retain others. In general, an outcome of a good training process is that executives learn who can and can't sell in the new model.

If I had the ear of CEO John Vaunt, I would advise him to stop using Anna Tucker as a troubleshooter and personally attend to the three challenges I've outlined. If he's hoping to build long-term competitive advantage, these issues deserve his attention. Cross selling usually generates higher margins, uses less capital per dollar of sales, and enables longer and deeper customer relationships. Such improvements boost the company's price/earnings ratio, but that's only the beginning. Consider GE Aircraft Engines, which adopted a solutions approach—combining engines, service, parts, and even financing—more than a decade ago. Its experience shows that if you package your product in the context of a well-delivered solution (in GE's case, the best value per dollar of investment), you have a great chance of selling the next generation of product (as happened in April when GE was one of two winners of the contracts for Boeing's 7E7 Dreamliner engines). Given how huge the lifetime value of a customer can be, higher retention is a true competitive advantage.

➢ Caroline A. Kovac

Caroline A. Kovac is the general manager of IBM Healthcare and Life Sciences in Somers, New York. She has worldwide responsibility for the strategic direction and day-to-day operations of IBM's health care and life sciences business.

Selling to a large enterprise with a complex hierarchy requires a lot of relationship building, both formal and informal. It takes time for a vendor to understand a customer's business, especially how to integrate new offerings so that they can deliver the highest value. Suppliers involved in this kind of relationship building are the farmers of the vendor world—they have to tend, water, and fertilize their accounts before they make a pitch. The vendors that target smaller, fast-moving companies are the hunters, always chasing down new deals. Their customers decide very quickly whether to buy, and the hunters move on. Consultants are analogous to farmers, while salespeople are more like hunters.

But the landscape is changing. Customers, for the most part, are no longer looking at tech for tech's sake. CEOs want vendors to help them solve complex business prob-

---

TopTek's consultants must broaden their knowledge and gain a deeper understanding of the firm's products and technologies.

---

lems, a situation that presents a challenge for TopTek. Its consultants complain that the sales force lacks an understanding of their clients' needs and is mainly interested in pushing product. The sales force thinks the consultants don't sell even their own services very effectively and don't care at all about product.

What both sides seem to have missed is that TopTek is no longer a consulting company or a products company. It has reinvented itself around the idea of solutions. The CEO needs to state TopTek's new value proposition, which has two parts: We understand our clients' problems better than anybody else, and we can bring our products and services to bear on those problems. This new reality will require changes in the roles and responsibilities people had before TopTek acquired Rossberg Lee.

The company's consultants must learn to broaden their knowledge beyond traditional services such as providing guidance in change management or business processes and strategies. With a solutions focus, they must be able to recommend not only what the client should implement but also how an implementation should occur. Doing so will require a deeper understanding of TopTek's various products and technologies than they now have.

Likewise, the sales force must adopt a solutions approach, which means learning more about clients' businesses and industries. Salespeople also must work closely with consultants so that together they can provide higher value by integrating products and services. Further, TopTek's compensation scheme must reward contributions to solutions delivery more than it does sales.

Good salespeople like Charlie are aware of the breadth of their company's offerings; consultants like Tricia know how the customer's business works. If the two groups can work together and acquire a bit of each other's skills, they'll have happier clients that in the end will buy more.

Some of our large accounts at IBM have had both an account team and a relationship with one of our consulting groups. At some point, we said, "We're going to put you together. Your job is to do the right thing for clients and solve their big problems while identifying opportunities for us. You will each bring different strengths, but you've got to be in this together."

This kind of involvement with clients' needs is deeper than cross selling, a term that's often interpreted to mean "If a customer likes this, maybe it'll like that." A year or two ago, Celera Genomics selected IBM as its technology provider. One reason Celera chose us was that we had invested in understanding the company's business needs, which went beyond product. They were impressed by our ability to integrate systems, including a storage product that wasn't one of our own. The client sets the direction. In our experience, the combination of deep industry and product knowledge is unbeatable. It could set TopTek apart and help the company solve its customers' toughest business problems.

➢ Jerome A. Colletti

Jerome A. Colletti (jerry@collettifiss.com) is the managing partner of Colletti-Fiss, a Scottsdale, Arizona-based management consulting firm specializing in sales effectiveness. He is a coauthor of Compensating New Sales Roles *(second edition, Amacom Books, 2001).*

John Vaunt is undoubtedly right that TopTek will have to change the way it rewards its account reps and Solutions consultants for sales. He should heed Anna's advice, however, and start by addressing more immediate issues. First, Peter Lee and Ron Murphy must establish a shared understanding of job roles and performance expectations in their organizations.

John's first step should be to convene a meeting with Anna, Peter, and Ron. The first item on the agenda should be Anna's findings from the project John gave her. But the larger purpose should be to begin the process of pulling together the legacy TopTek and legacy Rossberg Lee people into an effective customer-facing team.

TopTek's strategy of pursuing growth through sales of total solutions requires an approach that is fundamentally different from the way the two firms sold before. John's charge to Peter and Ron should be to figure out what is the right sales and customer relationship management process for the new TopTek. That process should make clear how new business will be acquired and how current business will be retained and expanded. It should explicitly address questions such as: Who is responsible for winning new accounts? Who is responsible for selling incremental business to current accounts? Going forward, what will be TopTek's sales approach for "small" products (like products and services for facilities management)? Should we continue the current practice of allowing practice leaders to sell their business or should we reassign that sales responsibility to our account executives?

As Peter and Ron go off to work on this assignment, John should indicate to them that Anna is available to facilitate their sessions and identify other resources (internal and external) to help them. He should also encourage Peter and Ron to involve their key people in the effort, to increase ownership in the new process. Finally, he should be very clear about when this work is due. It would not be unrealistic to ask for a high-level outline of the sales and customer relationship management process and a clarification of job accountabilities in 30 to 45 calendar days.

On a separate track, John should give Anna the task of identifying best practices in sales compensation among businesses like TopTek. This information will be useful when the team decides what new behaviors are required of salespeople and consultants and how those people can best be motivated.

Successful sales compensation plans are designed to the specific accountabilities of each job. It may be fully appropriate to continue rewarding account reps through a commission plan. However, a revised commission system might include new features such as sales quotas, minimum sales standards (to address what might be called the "annuity" feature in the present plan), and product or service mix objectives. Also, it may be wise to introduce bonuses for the consultants based on their involvement in sales. That's a common approach in companies where solutions consultants have a sales role.

Once the process is clear and accountabilities are assigned, TopTek's executives will have a much easier time moving forward with rethinking the compensation plan. There will be a framework for making decisions about performance measures, goals, and sales crediting—important ingredients in a sound compensation plan. With job accountabilities clear, it will be simpler to determine what training makes sense for both account reps and consultants. If it is necessary to hire new account reps, that too will be easier. Finally, internal and external customer communications can center on the sales process, so that the kind of confusion TopTek experienced at DigiDeal can be minimized or eliminated.

➤ Federico Turegano

Federico Turegano (federico.turegano@sgcib.com) is the managing director of SG Corporate and Investment Banking, an arm of Société Générale Group. He is also deputy head of the company's client management division in the Americas, based in New York.

Those of us in financial services tend to think our industry is unlike any other, but reading this dialogue almost makes me think someone has been listening in on my company's meetings. My organization has a similar structure to TopTek's, with "coverage bankers" (client relationship managers) on one side and specialists representing the various business lines—equity capital markets, project finance, export finance, and so forth—on the other side. And profitable growth for us depends heavily on success in cross selling.

A classic example of cross selling comes up when a specialized team executes a complex transaction—say, financing a power plant in Uzbekistan. The Project Finance team has its hands full pulling together all the required information for the transaction; how do we make sure its members will also bear in mind that there are other ways their bank can be of service? Turbines will have to be imported into the country, for example, so there's an export finance transaction to be done. And to the extent that those turbines have to be financed externally, there is a currency swap and perhaps an interest rate swap. Today, because of the pressure to produce profitable returns and leverage cost bases, we can't afford to miss these opportunities.

Capturing more of this business begins with a basic organizational step: putting product teams and client teams in frequent contact so that they constantly share up-to-date information. In our case, ensuring a fully transparent flow of information means frequent meetings (preferably short ones), the sharing of pipeline reports, and candid dialogue about the identification of client needs and new prospects.

What makes the most difference, however, is training. Products evolve rapidly—yes, even in banking—and we spend an enormous amount of time educating our coverage bankers about them. Often, the setting is informal. Five or six bankers might gather over lunch to hear from a business line about, for example, a new tax ruling and its impact or how tax-efficient financings such as so-called "green leases" can benefit certain clients. The goal is to enable the bankers to detect opportunities and then carry the ball for the first few yards. Our product line professionals, with their highly specialized knowledge, are a scarce resource. If one of them is brought to a client and, after five minutes, discovers that the product isn't relevant because of a tax situation or a legal constraint or a structural issue, then everyone's time has been wasted.

More generally, training must focus on building both sides' understanding of their respective jobs, perspectives, and time frames. One has a longer-term, global view of client relationships; the other has a more immediate, transactional view. The coverage banker's job is to ensure that the client has access to all the bank's products and that all the products have access to the client. But he needs to realize that, in playing the traffic-cop role, he may look like a roadblock to some of his colleagues. The product line professionals, for their part, need to appreciate the source of that caution. Once a product is delivered, the invoice is paid and that business line often exits the scene. But if it was oversold or underperforms, the coverage banker has to live with the consequences—and they will affect his ability to sell the next product.

TopTek management needs to manage the tension between these camps but at the same time recognize that some friction is inevitable—and not necessarily a bad thing. If I were John Vaunt, I would not try to engineer ideal behavior by tweaking compensation. Instead, I would engender a better cross selling environment through training, increased dialogue, and public recognition of cross selling successes, while tackling the cases of extreme dysfunction.

Originally published in July–August 2004

Reprint R0407B

A Rose by Any
Other Name

Executive Summary

Tom Rose had a lot on his plate. He was about to listen to his marketing head, Cassie Martin, make a major presentation on the biggest strategic initiative in Rose Partyware's history: the launch of a branded line of party ware.

Rose had manufactured paper goods for parties and other social events for many years. But Tom had recently spotted an opportunity to break out of the pack: a new printing technology that would improve quality and reduce costs. When Rose test-marketed the new line, consumers loved it, and retailers pledged their support. Tom felt that the new technology would give Rose the edge it needed to establish its own brand, which would in turn allow the company to stay ahead of its rivals.

In her presentation, Cassie reported that customers loved the brand concept. However, it was going to be more expensive than she had originally thought. So she recommended that the additional expenditure be funded with a small increase in the price of the proposed products. And Hank Lewis, Rose's national accounts manager, further complicated matters when he told Tom that one of Rose's biggest customers, Party!, had just decided to offer customers a complete line of party goods under its own name and wanted Rose to manufacture it. If the Party! store brand caught on, other retailers might follow suit. In that case, Rose would be the supplier of choice.

The management team is split on whether Rose should launch its own line or not. Tom needs to decide: What's the best marketing strategy for Rose Partyware?

Commentators Frank Weise III, Cott CEO; Micky Pant, Reebok chief marketing officer; Stephen J. Hoch, a marketing professor at Wharton; Judith Corstjens, head of Cubiculum Consultancy; and Marcel Corstjens, a marketing professor at Insead, offer advice in this fictional case study.

Tom Rose hated to go to a meeting with ice cream on his pants. But Rose Partyware's after-school party—a monthly gesture of goodwill to the local community and, not incidentally, a field trial for products the company was developing—had confirmed his suspicions that one of the new ice-cream bowls was just too shallow. The five-year-old who had demonstrated that fact had been sitting right next to him.

So here he was getting ready to listen to a major presentation, with paper towels in his hands. "Go ahead, Cassie," Tom said to his marketing director. "It'll dry or harden—or something. Thankfully, it's my last meeting of the day!"

He could tell that Cassie Martin was excited about the presentation she was going to make to the top management team. Tom had personally recruited her about a year ago to spearhead the biggest strategic initiative in Rose's history: the launch of a branded line of party ware. In fact, it was the first time a company in the party goods industry had contemplated a branding effort, at least in the 30 years Rose had been in business.

Party Lines

Rose manufactured a wide variety of paper goods—plates, bowls, cups, napkins, tablecloths, favors, crepe-paper streamers, and so forth—for birthday and holiday parties and other social events. Tom's uncle, who had worked for one of the largest paper companies in the United States, had started Rose in the 1970s. He had personally driven the company's growth until eight years ago, when he died suddenly, victim of an automobile accident.

A few years before the tragedy, Tom had joined the company—never expecting to stay long. He was freshly graduated from a liberal arts college and intended to work for a year while considering options for graduate school. Because he'd minored in art, Tom chose to work in Rose's design and graphics department. But as the year wore on and turned into another year, he was drawn more and more to the management issues Rose faced. His uncle soon had him spending time in the field, going on sales calls to better understand the needs of parents and brides and grooms to be, as well as those of the shop owners who helped make their parties happen. Before long, Tom was making his mark in Rose's sales department and was clearly being groomed to take on more responsibility.

When the company's patriarch and chairman suddenly passed away, the Rose family found itself turning again and again to Tom, the only family member who worked for the company. As they slowly absorbed the shock, a consensus emerged that he should take over the top slot. Tom reluctantly agreed. He persuaded his college roommate, Jerry Davis, who was then working for one of the country's largest accounting firms on the West Coast, to join him as chief financial officer but otherwise left the senior management team unchanged.

After a challenging first year learning the ropes as head of the company, Tom got Rose back onto the growth path disrupted by his uncle's tragic death. Over the next five years, he helped it realize annual gains in revenues and profits. That was not an easy achievement in the party goods industry, which was one of the last frontiers of entrepreneurship. Hundreds of small companies sold full party-ware lines or a few specialty products at throwaway prices, and new competitors appeared and disappeared regularly. They all competed for the attention of mass retailers, drugstore chains, and big regional grocers, as well as for independent retailers that sold party products through storefronts, catalogs, home-based distributors, and Web sites. The independents ranged in size from a few superstore chains with many outlets focused solely on party supplies to lots of owner-managed single stores that got by on sales of a few thousand dollars a month. Rose, with its high-end printing capabilities and great trade relations, was one of a handful of big players in the industry. It employed 300 people in its single plant and distribution centers around the country, and it was a pillar of the upstate New York town where it was headquartered.

Brand-New Capabilities

It was during a visit to Drupa, the German printing and paper trade fair, that Tom spotted his opportunity to break out of the pack. A vendor at the show was talking up its next-generation digital imaging technology, which took color files from the pre-press network and put them directly onto the printing press, thereby eliminating the expensive filmmaking process. That approach was still in prototype, but it held out the promise of speeding up production, making shorter print runs viable, and bringing down costs. Best of all, Tom thought, it might actually enhance the printed product's quality.

He decided to go with his hunch, and with the help of some expert consulting engineers, his production team modified the new machines to work with some of the trickier—and more eye-popping—inks and finishes. The results proved to be better than Tom had hoped: Abstract designs on the party ware seemed to glow, and popular characters, like Harry Potter and Frodo Baggins, acquired a near three-dimensional effect. When Rose test-marketed the new party-ware designs, consumers loved them, and all participating retailers said they would give the new line a lot of display and merchandising support.

That emboldened Tom, who had become increasingly concerned about the fact that Rose sold its party ware under generic labels like Your Birthday, Your Wedding, and Your Anniversary. The company's name—*his* name—appeared only on a small sticker on the back of the plastic packaging, almost as an informational afterthought. Tom felt that the new line presented a great opportunity to undertake a major branding effort. Having a strong brand, rooted in a quality advantage, would allow Rose to stay ahead of its rivals even when, sooner or later, they caught up with its printing capabilities.

When Tom asked around at conferences and trade shows about a person to lead his branding initiative, Cassie's name kept cropping up. People praised not just her creativity but also her business grounding: She had left a fast-track career in a market research firm to get her MBA. After B school, she joined a high-end toy-store chain, Toy Pile, and was credited with turning it into one of the top five in the industry.

Everything's Coming Up Roses

Tom was now seeing the evidence that his instincts had been right; Cassie's slides told a great story. She'd spent the better part of a year putting together Rose's fledgling marketing department and preparing for the launch of the branded line. She had researched customers, trade partners, and retail chains and established relationships with advertising and market research agencies, promotion houses, and merchandising firms. Customers loved the brand concept, Cassie was able to report with authority. They saw it as bringing a trust factor to party ware—as Crayola had done to crayons and Elmer's to glue.

"Virtually all our retailers, too, responded positively," crowed Cassie, as she moved on to the next slide. "The party stores and retail chains saw branding as bringing order and excitement to what is pretty much a hodgepodge today. The independents loved the idea of advertising behind a brand they could feature."

"The only bad news," Cassie continued, "is that establishing our brand is going to be more expensive than I had budgeted for. After conducting the advertising and promotion tests, we've found that we need to deliver the message more often in the first two years. In the toy business, I could concentrate communications around the holiday season. To make a party goods brand click in people's minds, we have to appear in a variety of magazines—for parents, brides, teens, and more—throughout the year. We have to grab people whenever they're thinking about throwing a party." Cassie passed the ad agency's creative presentation around the table to all the meeting members. Most of the group had seen one or two of the ads, but the reality of the full campaign created an instant buzz.

"My recommendation would be to fund this additional expenditure with a small price increase on all the branded items." She put up a new slide. "As you can see, my figures show that we should be able to accomplish our objectives with a price hike in the range of 6% to 7%. In your presentation books, after the cost estimates, I have included studies of half-a-dozen brands that sell at premiums to nonadvertised competitors and still lead their markets. Our price differential would be less than all those cases."

"I don't know about that, Cassie." It was Jerry Davis, the CFO. "Party ware has always been a commodity business, and pricing above the market scares me. When people are hurriedly comparing paper items for a party, they will always opt for the cheaper product."

"Customers say that isn't true," Cassie countered. She switched to a slide that underscored the point. "In our studies, they consistently indicated that they were willing to pay even more for our branded products than I'm suggesting."

"What they say can be different from what they do," Jerry replied. "Sure, they'll take a stand on quality when speaking to a researcher, but when they're buying disposable stuff for 20 little kids, it's easy to say, 'Who'll notice the difference?'"

Tom interceded. "Jerry, you've put your finger on a key decision point. But I want to give everyone a chance to digest what Cassie's presented. As you know, we're reconvening next week to wrestle this to the ground." He thanked Cassie for her excellent presentation and adjourned the meeting.

A Thorny Issue

As Tom made his way back to his office, his national accounts manager, Hank Lewis, caught up with him. "Got a minute?" he asked.

"This may complicate things a bit," Hank said, as he shut Tom's office door behind him. "Remember I was out calling on Party! yesterday?" He was referring to one of Rose's largest customers. "I got back just in time for Cassie's presentation. The thing is, Party! has decided to get into private labeling in this category. It's planning to offer customers a complete line of party goods under its own name."

Seeing Tom wince, Hank hastened to continue. "Yeah, that's the bad news. But the good news is, they want us to do the production. They'd just be doing the designing and setting the specs."

"But that's not our business, Hank," Tom replied, a little sharply. "We've always been marketers and designers, not just pressmen."

"Better listen to the full story," advised Hank. "Party! is going to do this with or without us. The company plans to give its store line lots of space and merchandising support and sharply reduce the number of other party-ware lines it carries. If we're the supplier, we're guaranteed one of the remaining positions. If we're not, there are no guarantees. I don't need to remind you that's about 20% of our sales."

Having Tom's full attention now, Hank filled in more details. The retailer, he reported, would initially test the line in 100 of its stores. If it did well, the company would roll it out to all 300 outlets. "Party! will price the products on a par with the other lines, including ours, but it's proposing to pay us 15% less than it does now. Still, we wouldn't have to spend any promotional dollars on those sales, and the volumes could be huge. The price difference and the promotional spending about balance out, and, net-net, I figure it would be a good-sized win for us."

"Okay," countered Tom, "but you're not thinking of our setup costs to do it. And it sounds to me like you're counting on sales of our own lines holding steady. Won't Party! be cannibalizing a lot of them?"

Hank pressed the case again. "No question, Party! will be a gorilla of a rival, but like I said, the stores will carry fewer other lines. I think we could hold our own," he said, getting up to go. "Maybe even do a little better."

Behind Every Successful Brand

As Tom drove home that night, it struck him that he faced an either-or proposition; Rose didn't have the capacity, he was sure, to undertake Cassie's branding initiative and respond to the Party! opportunity at the same time.

Lost in thought, he nearly forgot the promise he'd made to his daughter to pick up supplies for her school project. He ended up backtracking a mile to Office-Mart rather than going home without the requisite three colors of poster board and markers.

On his way to the register, Tom stopped short in front of a section devoted to writing tablets. Six brands were on display, but the top shelf and the two bottom rows all bore the same name: OfficeMart. Tom also saw a neat display of OfficeMart scratch pads when he got to the end of the notebook aisle and a stack of smaller OfficeMart notepads near the register. He thought back to something Hank had said as he left Tom's office: "You're always saying we should look for the opportunity in every setback. Maybe there's a bigger business for us in this private-label stuff than just this one account."

It was hard to argue with Hank's assertion. If the Party! store brand caught on, all the other mass and party chains might want to launch private-label brands, too, and quickly. In that case, Rose could be the supplier of choice—the one that had already figured out how to do it and represented the lowest-risk partner.

The next morning, Tom decided his first conversation should be with Marge Dinson, Rose's sales director for the independent stores. In truth, his heart had always been with this group, the small retailers who focused on providing their customers with a little more personalized service along with their party-ware purchases. They were an idiosyncratic bunch: mothers looking for a career after the kids had left home, caterers and liquor distributors who sold party goods as an important adjunct to their businesses, some Internet-only sellers—all were great sources of ideas and encouragement. Tom always looked forward to meeting these folks at the shows and in their shops; he felt he owed them a debt of gratitude for Rose's success over the years.

Tom and Marge met over a cup of coffee in his office, where he proceeded to explain the Party! opportunity to her. It didn't take long to tell where Marge stood on it. "Madness!" she cut in, as soon as she got the gist of it. "This industry is like a small town, and the day any retail chain launches its own line, by 5 PM everyone will know who's making it. That's a loyalty check. Every party store, every supermarket, every drugstore is trying to eat the independents' lunch. You're either with 'em or against 'em. They realize we can't stop selling to the chains, but they sure don't expect us to make the wave that could wash them away. You'd lose 80% of their business in the first six months. That's almost 35% of our sales. You'll be better off telling the independents what Party! is planning and asking them to ratchet up their support for our products than turning the screw on them yourself. And you really think they'll get behind our branded line if we also manufacture products for Party!? Forget it."

What's in a Name?

The next day, the management team once again gathered in the party room; Tom had asked Hank to present Party!'s proposal to all the group members, after which they would hear Marge's point of view. Both Hank and Marge got caught up in their emotions and went further than either had earlier.

"Whether we like it or not, chains are the future," Hank declared. "We had better learn how to play their game, or we're going to be on the sidelines with a handful of independents, making a futile last stand. This business is changing, and we have to change with it."

"Hank, you've been living with those chains for so long, you've bought their story completely," Marge shot back. "The fact is, you simply can't trust them. Today, you'll be their favorite. Tomorrow, they'll want to pay you a dime less on their line, then a dollar less. You're not at the foot of a ladder; instead, you're at the top of a slippery slope."

The rest of the group didn't hold back, either. Jack Kuczinski, Rose's production manager for almost two decades, reminded Tom that they were in possession of a printing breakthrough. "Anyone can be a commodity producer," Jack stated flatly. "If your uncle had wanted to be in that business, he'd have stayed at United Paper. But the fact is, we manufacture products better than anyone else does. There's no way any retailer is going to toss us out of their stores. This branding thing is the way to go, if you ask me. It's about pride in who and what we are—not skulking around like the man behind the curtain. I bet that every person on the shop floor feels exactly the same way."

Charlotte Hann, the design director and another company veteran, seconded those thoughts. "We can do exciting things with both designs and the brand, but we won't have any impact—and I expect no one in the company will feel very proud—if we use someone else's brand."

"Sorry to be the party pooper here," said Jerry, jumping in. "But we're trying to choose between two bad ideas. On the branding issue, you simply have to scale it back to a point where our products can be competitively priced. A disaster awaits any premium-priced product in this market, whatever the reason for the higher price. As for Party!'s offer, I think we should pass. If it succeeds and we're part of it, it has a relationship downside in every other segment of our market. If it fails and we're part of it, the damage is even worse. Hank's numbers look good today, but once we get pressured to cut prices and have lost a chunk of the independents' business, we will be in trouble. I think this is a time to be careful."

The last speaker was Cassie, who summarized the key points from her earlier meeting, emphasizing her confidence that a branded line would be a major success. She was clearly disappointed that the team members doubted it would work. "Every test we carried out says that a brand can succeed," she repeated. "The rewards for being the first to brand will be tremendous for Rose—not just in terms of sales but also in the consolidation of our position with both customers and the trade. In the toy industry, companies with powerful brands call the shots. Commodity producers come and go."

She had plenty more to say as she walked back to her office with Tom. "I don't think that the branding opportunity will last forever, Tom," Cassie explained. "People are going to be talking about the fact that Rose has been doing research in this area, and someone is going to do it sooner or later. If it's not us, I'm sad, and it'll mean that there won't be much of a role for me here. Your sales guys can handle the maintenance ad and promotion spending—and that's pretty much all it will be—without me and my salary."

Rose on the Fence

Four weeks later, Tom was on a plane to Party!'s headquarters. On his laptop were two PowerPoint presentations. One explained why he was excited about Party!'s plans to launch a store brand and how Rose's lines could grow in tandem with it. The other argued that

Rose's new branded line was important enough for Party! to hold off on its test launch and evaluate the impact of Rose's branded line on its sales before making a final decision. As the plane taxied down the runway, Tom was still not sure how he'd lead off.

What's the Best Marketing Strategy for Rose Partyware?

Five commentators offer expert advice.

➤ Frank E. Weise III

Frank E. Weise III is the chairman, president, and chief executive officer of Cott, based in Toronto.

If I were Tom Rose, I'd be excited by the opportunities for my business, not worried about the threat from retailer brands. I would partner with my large retailer customers to better understand their unique channel propositions in the party-ware category and try to develop products that would result in higher sales and profits both for retailers and my company.

Tom must realize that the U.S. retailing industry is in the middle of a major consolidation. As the big retailers become more powerful, they will continue to brand the shopping experience as well as the products they sell. Retailer brands offer the chains a way to differentiate themselves and develop direct relationships with consumers. Because they deliver the same or greater value at cheaper prices, most customers love them. Retailer brands are also more profitable for chains to carry. In the food industry, they typically deliver 10% higher gross margins to retailers than na-

---

Tom must realize that the U.S. retailing industry is in the middle of a major consolidation.

---

tional brands do. That's why chains like Loblaws in Canada and Wal-Mart in the United States have created powerful retailer brands like President's Choice and Sam's Choice.

When choosing vendors, most retailers treat price as just one of several factors. They prefer to tie up with companies that can add value to their operations in three ways. First, most retailers look for suppliers that can develop new products, better packaging, and merchandising and promotion tools. Second, they value vendors that can manage the entire supply chain, down to the store-level inventory. Finally, they expect suppliers to manage the category for them by developing a deep understanding of the consumer. Such category managers not only forecast demand trends but also anticipate the optimal shelf layouts and off-shelf merchandising opportunities across the chain.

Because Rose is a market leader, Tom should propose that Party! appoint his company the party-ware category manager. He should suggest the creation of a party zone of dedicated retail shelf space in every store to bring order to the category. Shoppers make 80% of their purchase decisions at the point of sale—42% of them in five seconds or less—so a focused display will enhance sales. Tom should also position this proposal as a cost-savings opportunity since the party zone would allow Party! to reduce the number of competing lines and assortments of party ware it currently carries. Finally, Rose should offer to manage the chain's party-ware inventory and promotions, the latter on a monthly and, if consumer differences warrant it, regional basis.

As Tom will discover, category management will bring his company several intangible benefits. For instance, I suspect that Rose will discover that it makes a lot of commodity products that sell only on the basis of price and are ideal candidates for retailer branding. But Tom will find that he can brand certain noncommodity products and charge premium prices. In those cases, Rose could create multiple brands and segment them by distribution channel, key customer, or usage such as birthdays and weddings. Consumers will be willing to spend more on wedding party supplies than they would for, say, holiday party goods.

However, Rose should focus squarely on packaging design, which influences consumer purchasing decisions. I would not recommend a large marketing investment elsewhere—in a national brand-creation program, for example—because of the category's size and the company's limited resources. A big branding effort is also unlikely to reach the intended target audience because Rose sells its products through so many different distribution channels.

Tom will also need to educate his senior executives about his new vision for the business. He must talk to them about the retail market's changing dynamics, the need for category management, and the importance of working closely with Rose's retail customers. Change, I believe, brings opportunity to those who can see it.

➤ Micky Pant

Micky Pant is the chief marketing officer of Reebok International, based in Canton, Massachusetts.

I say, go with Cassie Martin. Tom should create a brand and invest in its development. It may seem like a risky thing for a small company to do, but the alternatives are even riskier.

Tom will hear three standard arguments against brand building. First, he will be told that branding is not important when it comes to party ware because most people don't buy such products on a regular basis. Second, it will be argued that building brand awareness will cost the company a great deal of money and that Rose's rivals will outprice it in the short run. Third, Tom's critics will point out that large retailers would never allow a supplier trying to build its brand to use premium pricing, so Rose will lose revenues in the near term. However, those arguments will prove false in the long run.

I know of no product category for which branding is unimportant. Every year produces more and more businesses that have been built by branding what used to be commodities. Brands offer the comfort of familiarity in an increasingly hostile world, and humble paper cups and plates are no exception. If I remember right, one of the earliest examples of successful branding in the paper industry was Scott Paper's branding of toilet tissue—surely a less deserving candidate for branding than party ware. Hallmark has brought familiarity to printed stationery and is able to charge a premium for its products. And parties are usually happy occasions, where consumers will happily spend that extra 7% to do things right.

It is going to be expensive for Rose to create a brand, but it needn't be prohibitively so. Tom would do well to remember that advertising isn't the only way to build awareness. The most important branding vehicle is the product itself. The intelligent development of the brand name and innovative uses of the logo can work surprisingly well. A logo, cleverly applied to the product, will serve as a brand ambassador at every party. I would also concentrate on developing unique product packaging and point-of-sale display materials. These aren't expensive, and they can be used to build a base of consumer awareness.

Tom must remember that retailers are the enemies of brands and brand building. In their eyes, brands waste money fighting each other, and that does them little good. As long as store traffic increases, retailers couldn't care less which brand consumers buy. They overemphasize the importance of pricing and forever seek larger discounts and margins from suppliers. A supplier can build a strong business by maintaining a direct relationship with consumers, over retailers' heads. The only way to curb retail power is to build the strength of your brand.

Rose will be shooting itself in the foot if it helps build Party!'s brand, although Tom may make some money in the short run. As the retailer's brand gains strength, Rose will be pressured to reduce its margins. Tom will have to rely on technological innovations, like the printing process he recently invested in, for the company's survival, but they're no guarantee. Branding would be the flywheel that maintains the company's momentum in times of little innovation or falling demand.

Tom needn't, of course, alienate his largest customer. He should explore how the two companies can best work together rather than present a definite course of action. Since the details of Rose's branding project haven't been finalized, Tom need only mention the project to Party!'s top management. But he should honestly tell that company how concerned he is about getting marginalized once Party! launches its private-label brand.

Tom should empower Cassie to launch a branded line of party ware, although he must warn Jerry to prevent any profligate ad spending. There will be bumps along Rose's road to a branded future, but at least the journey will have begun.

➢ Stephen J. Hoch

Stephen J. Hoch is the John J. Pomerantz Professor and the chair of the marketing department at the University of Pennsylvania's Wharton School of Business in Philadelphia. He is the coeditor, with Howard Kunreuther, of Wharton on Making Decisions *(John Wiley & Sons, 2001).*

When Tom Rose claims, "We've always been marketers and designers, not just pressmen," he's both right and wrong. He's right in that Rose has demonstrated the ability to design, print, and manufacture high-quality paper goods. That expertise has allowed the company to come up with a product line for which it may well be able to charge consumers a modest price premium. Rose could probably get away with that because of the new line's superior quality and the company's emphasis on selling its products through independent stores, where less price-sensitive consumers usually shop.

Still, Tom is mostly wrong when he says that Rose has become a marketer over the decades. There is little evidence the company has developed a core competence in building brands and creating promotions. Until now, Rose appears to have relied almost entirely on the push from its retailer customers—who are closer to the consumer than Rose is—to boost sales. In fact, Rose may not have the market power to foist a higher price for its branded line on its retailers. So, while Cassie might be able to create a brand, it probably won't have the equity Tom desires.

The benefits of creating a brand in the party-ware category aren't obvious, and that's why none of Rose's rivals have been able to pull it off. Another reason is that it is expensive for companies to maintain "top of mind" awareness for unpredictable product purchases. For instance, while holiday parties take place at certain times of the year, other kinds can happen at any time. So party-ware producers like Rose have no choice but to depend on retailers to have products at the right place at the right time.

Tom should move into the private-label business, particularly since it's not very different from selling national brands with low name recognition. By doing so, Rose will gain some additional clout with Party!, if nothing else, due to the procurement efficiencies that the retailer will generate by dealing with just one vendor. Tom can use that to convince the chain to continue carrying the no-name party-ware products his company makes. As Rose's interests become more similar to Party!'s, they will be better able to coordinate their efforts.

The key decision Tom needs to make in this context has to do with product quality. My research suggests that the only way to go is the high-quality route. Retailers sell more private-label products, make more money, and build their own brand equity by selling top-quality merchandise. Tom must convince Party! that it is in everyone's interest to have high-quality specs and creative designs. If the retailer myopically insists on cheap, low-quality products, he should pass on Party!'s offer and take the idea to some of the other large retailers.

Tom cannot protect the independent retailers. Consolidation in the retailing industry is inevitable as the shakeouts in grocery and drug retailing clearly show. But the independents will not disappear overnight, and they need something to keep Rose's products fresh and exciting. Investing in relatively inexpensive brand-building efforts, such as better packaging and point-of-sale displays, will allow Tom to offer added value to the independents, who are bound to feel betrayed by his decision to produce Party!'s line.

If Rose had already established a strong national-brand presence, I'd have said that Tom should stick to the knitting, continue to invest in high-quality products, and let someone else make the private-label product. I don't know of too many instances of national-brand manufacturers supplying the private label to retailers, even though most of them have toyed with the idea. And I think they are right not to do so. The economics of the brands and private labels differ, and the emphasis that the organization must place on new-product development and brand building would have to change as a result. That's why most big pharmaceutical companies left the generics business after investing heavily in that market in the early 1990s.

➤ Judith Corstjens and Marcel Corstjens

Judith Corstjens runs Cubiculum Consultancy in London, and Marcel Corstjens is the Unilever Chaired Professor of Marketing at Insead in Fontainebleau, France. They are the coauthors of Store Wars: The Battle for Mindspace and Shelfspace *(John Wiley & Sons, 1999).*

Tom Rose has dithered over launching a branded line of party ware and is now dallying over becoming a private-label contractor. It is time for Tom to justify his family's faith in him by displaying more decisive leadership. He can dismiss the notions of doing both or doing nothing. Collaborating with Party! to create a line of private-label products and, at the same time, launching a branded line is not realistic. Tom doesn't have the resources to do both projects justice.

Moreover, Party! has approached Rose because it wants to create a premium private label; had the retailer wanted to sell party ware at rock-bottom prices, it would have gone to a supplier in Asia. If Party! and Rose simultaneously launch branded lines, they will end up competing for the same consumer, and they will compromise the success of both brands.

If Tom does nothing, he is leaving the door open for rivals to exploit both opportunities. He could later find himself trying to head off a concerted attempt at private-label development in a commodity market or watching regretfully as a rival threatens Rose's leadership by launching a pio-neering brand in the industry category.

While Tom has carefully researched the possibility of launching a branded line, he has not been as assiduous in his assessment of the opportunity that the private-label business presents. In fact, Rose's top management team's discussions were long on emotion and short on fact. Tom must remember that many business opportunities prom-ise high returns for the first entrant, but success attracts competition and reduces margins. Only if he believes that his company can sustain a cost advantage in the long run should he take it into the private-label business.

Hank's argument that a private-label supplier can nego-tiate, in return, more space and better displays for its brands in a retailer's stores is spurious. Retailers stock a brand only if the consumer demands it. It is also wrong to believe that producing extra volumes from spare capacity will make large, low-margin, private-label contracts prof-itable. Tom can never hope that his products will compete with the store brand if he falls for the retailer's logic and charges only the marginal cost for producing private-label products. Rose will also face a dilemma when spare capac-ity gets used up—when business picks up or machinery ages—and it needs to invest in fresh capacity.

Tom must launch Rose's own branded line. There is no point in creating a brand if it serves no real purpose for the consumer or if a private label can play that role just as well. But many brands were created against those very odds: Covent Garden in soups, Muller in yogurt, Tropicana in orange juice. Between Tom's concern for the consumer and Cassie's creativity and confidence, they seem to have what it takes to make a go of it.

Once Rose has revamped the party-ware category, retailers may launch private labels under its price umbrella. If Tom then wants to take up the private-label business, he should assess the opportunity as an independent endeavor. Managing the two businesses together would make it difficult for Rose to compete against suppliers that focus only on private labels, or just their own brands. Tom would do well to remember the fate of companies like United Biscuits, which fell victim to the phantom synergies between private-label and branded businesses.

We often see organizations get fixated on choosing the one best strategy. There is often no one superior strategy; several might lead to a sustainable advantage. Just as important as the strategy is the will behind it. Tom must consider the commitment he will get from his team for the strategy he chooses, and he would be more in line with the company's spirit if he chose the branding option. Investing in a direct link with the consumer is Tom's best chance to ensure that Rose is around to pay his pension.

Originally published in March 2003
Reprint R0303A

ABOUT THE CONTRIBUTORS

Ford Harding is the founder of Maplewood, New Jersey–based Harding & Company, which consults to professional firms on sales.

Paul Hemp is a senior editor at HBR.

Julia Kirby is editor, special issues, at HBR.

Walter Kuemmerle is an associate professor at Harvard Business School.

Daniel B. Stone is the vice president of corporate communications at Alberto-Culver in Melrose Park, Illinois.

John Strahinich, an editor for the *Boston Herald*, was formerly executive editor of both *Boston* magazine and *Boston Business Journal*.

Thomas J. Waite serves as a strategic adviser to numerous organizations.